First published by Parragon in 2009

Parragon
Queen Street House
4 Queen Street
Bath BA1 1HE, UK

Created and produced by

studio cactus ©

13 SOUTHGATE STREET WINCHESTER HAMPSHIRE SO23 9DZ

DESIGN Laura Watson, Sharon Rudd
EDITORIAL Jennifer Close

ISBN: 978-1-4075-5527-0

Printed in China

STUDIO CACTUS WOULD LIKE TO THANK
Sharon Cluett for original styling; Anthony Duke for range
maps; Claire Moore for introductory illustrations; Sharon Rudd
for Order silhouettes; Jo Weeks for proofreading; and
Penelope Kent for indexing

PICTURE CREDITS
All images © NHPA, except:
Andy Z 12 cl; Christian Musat 11 bl; easyshoot 12 brr; Ed
Phillips 12 bc; Ervin Monn 12 br; Getty Images 14, 74 t; Jason
Vandehey 12 cc; Karel Gallas 12 bl; Michael Woodruff 6; Mike
Danzenbaker 59 bl; pasphotography 12 bll; Photolibrary Group
19 t, 57 b, 66 t , 88 t; RLHambley 4 l; SouWest Photography 12
cr; Workmans Photos 12 crr.

COVER CREDITS: Main image: Bald Eagle Perched on a Branch
Holding a Fish © Getty Images. Right hand side/back image:
Sunset Behind Clouds © Gail Shumway / Getty Images. Bottom
left to right: Yellow Warbler © NHPA; Yellow-bellied Sapsucker
© Photolibrary Group; Indigo Bunting © Photolibrary Group

CONTENTS

ABOUT THIS BOOK

The way in which birds are grouped together is based on the same underlying principles that apply in other areas of the natural world. The classificatory system works through a series of ranks, which become increasingly more refined, allowing the individual birds to be recognized within this general framework.

BIRDS AND US

Attempts to evolve a classificatory system not just for birds but for all life forms began with the ancient Greeks, but the modern science of classification, called taxonomy, stems from the pioneering work of Swedish botanist and zoologist Carl Linnaeus in the middle of the 18th century.

This is not a static field, however, and the scientific names given to birds have changed quite frequently in the past. A major shift in our understanding of bird groups is now starting to occur, thanks to DNA studies, and this will finally establish avian relationships from a genetic rather than an anatomical viewpoint.

DISTRIBUTION MAPS

The maps in this book give an indication of where a particular species is most likely to be seen in North America. Migrants may occur over a wider area as they fly back and forth between their wintering and breeding grounds.

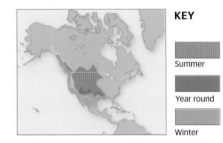

KEY

Summer

Year round

Winter

SYMBOLS IN THIS BOOK

The silhouettes give some indication of the profiles of the birds in particular Orders, although there can be marked divergences in a few cases, notably in the Piciformes, which embrace species ranging from woodpeckers to toucans. Each order consists of a number of families. Then below the family rank are the different genera. It is possible to orientate yourself within the classificatory tree by the way in which the names are written. Orders always end with -formes, as in the case of Columbiformes, while at Family level, the ending is -ae, as Columbidae. Genera are the first rank to be written in an italicized form, as in *Columba*. The species is a binomial (or two-part) name, as in the case of *Columba livia*, and, again, is always written in italics. Where there is a subspecies recognized, there will be a third name, such as *Columba livia livia*, marking the lowest level in the classificatory tree.

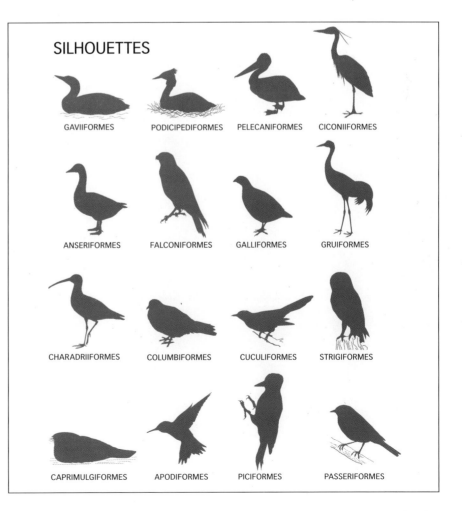

SILHOUETTES

GAVIIFORMES

PODICIPEDIFORMES

PELECANIFORMES

CICONIIFORMES

ANSERIFORMES

FALCONIFORMES

GALLIFORMES

GRUIFORMES

CHARADRIIFORMES

COLUMBIFORMES

CUCULIFORMES

STRIGIFORMES

CAPRIMULGIFORMES

APODIFORMES

PICIFORMES

PASSERIFORMES

WHAT ARE BIRDS?

Perhaps the most obvious characteristic associated with birds—an ability to fly—is actually not one of the features that separate them from other vertebrate groups. In fact, a number of birds such as penguins, kiwis and ostriches cannot fly, while on the other hand, mammals such as bats have mastered the power of flight. A distinguishing characteristic of birds is, however, their body covering. Feathers, which help to protect the body and insulate it, as well as providing an ability to fly, are only seen in birds. Another trait of birds is the way in which they reproduce: all species lay eggs with a hard calcareous ("chalk-like") shell.

ANCESTOR This is a fossil of *Archaeopteryx*, which is currently the world's oldest known bird. The distinctive claws on the wing tips can be seen here.

BIG BEGINNINGS Quetzalcoatlus had a wingspan approaching 40 ft (12 m). This pterosaur is therefore the largest creature yet discovered that possessed the power of flight. This reptile lacked any teeth in its narrow jaws and fed on small sea creatures.

THE ORIGINS OF BIRDS

Over the past decade, the origins of birds have become clearer, and many zoologists believe that they are descended from small dinosaurs, which evolved the ability to fly. They survived the mass extinction of their larger relatives that took place at the end of the Cretaceous era, some 65 million years ago, and soon became the dominant group of vertebrates possessing the power of flight. Birds rapidly diversified and spread around the world, replacing the pterosaurs, a reptilian group that had first taken to the skies about 130 million years previously.

Fossilized evidence of the early birds that would reveal the history of their development is sparse, compared with many dinosaurs. This is partly due to their much smaller size. Their bodies were more likely to be eaten by larger scavengers rather than being preserved in such a way that their remains would ultimately be fossilized. Nevertheless, a growing number of avian fossils have been unearthed over recent years, particularly in the area of present-day China, revealing more about how the group developed.

The earliest recognizable bird is still *Archaeopteryx*, whose remains were unearthed in a Bavarian slate quarry in Germany during 1861. Based on the age of the layer of rock in which the fossil was found, this bird died about 145 million years ago. *Archaeopteryx* had a similar appearance to modern birds, with recognizable feathers, and was able to fly rather than just glide from tree to tree.

It would appear that these early birds were far less agile on the wing than their descendants today. They were equipped with claws on their wing tips, which allowed them to clamber around on the branches. This characteristic is still evident in one species today—the South American Hoatzin (*Opisthocomus hoazin*—see box).

Hoatzin chicks

Like early bird ancestors, Hoatzin chicks hatch with claws on the tips of their wings. The nest is often built above water, but, thanks partly to their claws, if they fall in they can anchor on to vegetation and then climb back up to the nest site. These claws are shed as the chicks grow older and are able to start flying.

OSTRICH The bulk of the Ostrich (*Struthio camelus*) means that these avian giants cannot fly, relying instead on their powerful legs to outrun potential predators.

Early birds such as *Archaeopteryx* also had sharp teeth in their jaws. These gradually disappeared as the bird's skeleton lightened, enhancing its flying abilities. Seabirds hunting fish were seemingly the last group to lose their teeth, reflecting the difficulties of grasping their slippery prey. Gradually, however, the shape of their bills became modified to undertake this task efficiently.

Many of the avian families that are now in existence had already evolved around 38 million years ago. Fossils cannot show the colors of these early birds, but it is likely that seabirds were relatively dull, with black and white coloration predominating in their plumage, while forest species were probably more brightly colored.

EXTINCT GIANTS

The African Ostrich is the biggest bird on earth today, but there used to be other, even larger and far more ferocious species. These birds were all too large to fly, but they made up for this by their long-legged gait, which enabled them to move fast on land. The most fearsome group were the phororhacids that roamed from the southern United States down across South America and lived and hunted in flocks. They could grow to about 10 ft (3 m) tall and had powerful bills as well as sharp talons on their feet that allowed them to overpower their quarry easily.

AVIAN ANATOMY

Birds' front limbs have evolved into wings, and cannot be used for walking. As a result, their center of gravity differs from that of mammals: Their legs have been brought forward to support the weight of their bodies. A bird's wings are rather like those of an airplane, with flight being made possible by curvature over the upper surface. This lessens the air resistance here, compared with the underside, making it easier for the bird to take off and remain in the air.

BEATING WINGS The long feathers running along the back of the wing of this Bewick Swan (*Cygnus columbianus*) are the flight feathers, which provide the thrust that a bird needs to be able to become airborne.

Parts of a bird

Specific terms are used to describe the various areas of a bird's body, and assist in the identification of individual species by enabling differences in coloration or markings to be highlighted easily. These features can also help in terms of determining an individual's gender. More general descriptions may also be used, such as the underparts, which relates to the underside of the body, or the upperparts, running down over the back to the rump.

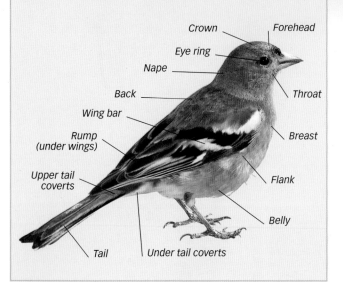

Crown
Forehead
Eye ring
Nape
Back
Throat
Wing bar
Rump (under wings)
Breast
Upper tail coverts
Flank
Belly
Tail
Under tail coverts

FLIGHT

Some birds such as condors use their wings to glide, relying on upward columns of warm air, known as thermals. This enables them to stay airborne without having to flap their wings frequently, providing an energy-efficient way of remaining airborne.

The angle of the wings affects the bird's movement, with flapping of the wings providing propulsive power. Well-developed chest muscles assist with this task. There are specialist flight feathers running along the back of each wing, whose position alters during the flight cycle. The most evident feathers are the flight feathers, running along the back edge of the bird's wings. The primary flight feathers, located toward the tips, are the longest, and provide thrust. They can move independently to adjust air resistance. The secondary flight feathers, closest to the body, are shorter, and help to give the bird lift in flight. With each downward thrust, the flight feathers are held together, helping the bird to climb. Once the bird wants to slow down, approaching a perch for example, then it simply glides down, ceasing to flap its wings, but adjusting their position to help to reach the branch. When it wants to slow down more quickly, the bird spreads its tail feathers, increasing air resistance and exerting a greater drag effect.

PLUMAGE

Birds rely on the body covering of feathers, described as their plumage, to keep warm as well as insuring that they can fly. The body itself is covered in soft, smooth contour feathers that cover its surface. These are organized in distinctive feather tracts, called pterylae.

Beneath these feathers can be a layer of down feathering, which helps maintain body temperature, trapping warm air close to the skin. This insulation is important because birds' body temperature generally averages between 106–110 degrees F (41 and 43.5 degrees C), and they have no body fat beneath their skin, unlike mammals. Apart from flying, however, birds use their feathers for other purposes too. In some cases, as with Tricolored Blackbirds (*Agelaius tricolor*), males will use their breeding plumage as part of their courtship display. The coloration of the feathers helps to distinguish the sexes easily in some cases throughout the year and also enables young birds to be recognized.

The plumage is kept in good condition by preening, using bills and occasionally claws. There are various parasites such as feather lice that may nibble at the feathers, and some birds treat themselves with a natural insecticide, smearing the formic acid from ants that they catch over their feathers. The plumage is usually shed on an annual basis, enabling frayed or damaged feathers to be replaced. Some birds, such as the striking Indigo Bunting (*Passerina cyanea*), molt at the start of the breeding season as well, growing more colorful or elaborate plumage for display purposes. Birds keep their plumage waterproof by smearing oil over the feathering. This is produced from the preen gland at the base of the tail.

SWIMMING All birds that spend large amounts of time in or on the water have webbed feet for more efficient paddling. This allows them to swim faster and with less effort. Birds that often dive and swim underwater, such as auks and guillemots, use front limbs as flippers. Propulsive power underwater is generated by their legs rather than their wings.

Flight

While the basic structure of the wing remains broadly identical, birds display a range of wing shapes, and these can give important clues as to their lifestyles. Birds such as swallows that spend much of their time in flight have angular wings and can fly with relatively little effort, gliding if needed. Other long-distance migrants such as curlews may have a similar wing structure, while the wing shape of kestrels enables them to hover, while they scan the ground below for prey. The wings of hummingbirds can be extended back behind the body, with the wing beats helping the bird to remain airborne, while at the same time, enabling it to hover and feed. This allows the hummingbird to move in close to the flower without its wings getting in the way. Pheasants, in contrast, are heavy birds, and not well adapted to flight. It takes considerably muscular effort for them to become airborne. Nevertheless, the rounded shape of their wings enables them to glide down smoothly when they spot a suitable area of cover. Vultures have long wings so they can remain airborne for long periods with minimal effort, gliding on columns of warm air known as thermals.

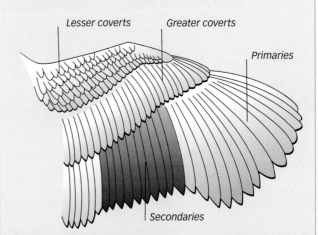

Lesser coverts   *Greater coverts*   *Primaries*   *Secondaries*

AN EXTENDED VIEW OF A BIRD'S WING, SEEN FROM ABOVE.

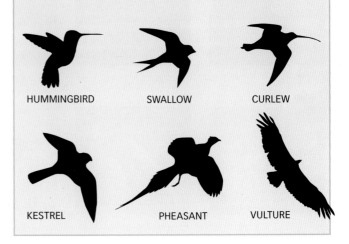

HUMMINGBIRD   SWALLOW   CURLEW

KESTREL   PHEASANT   VULTURE

FEEDING

Birds eat a wide variety of foodstuffs, with some species being carnivorous, while others are essentially herbivorous. The majority, however, will feed on a mixture of foods. Much can be learnt about the feeding habits of a particular species by the shape of its bill. Birds that feed on seeds, such as finches, tend to have a fairly sturdy, conical-shaped bill. This allows them to crack the outer casing of the seed and extract the kernel. Species that have narrow and relatively long bills are likely to feed largely on invertebrates, poking and probing to extract insects and spiders from their hiding places in bark, or using their bills to locate worms and oysters hidden in the sand at low tide.

Some birds have very specialized bills related to their method of feeding. Hummingbirds, which rely on flower nectar as a source of energy, have slender bills of varying shapes, to aid their ability to extract nectar from specific types of flowers growing in the areas where they occur.

Certain families of birds rely not just on their bills but also their feet to help feeding, holding food down on the perch and ripping off pieces that they can swallow easily. Such behavior is commonly seen in birds of prey, which also have sharp claws known as talons on their toes, enabling them to seize their quarry in the first instance.

SPECIALIZED HUNTERS Birds of prey have hooked bills, enabling them to rip their prey apart with relative ease. They also have strong feet, equipped with sharp, curved talons. This enables them to catch and carry heavy prey, such as the fish caught by this Osprey (*Pandion haliaetus*).

INTERNAL ANATOMY

The internal organs of birds reflect the demands of flight, and so are adapted accordingly, so as to minimize body weight. In the case of the digestive system, there are no teeth in the mouth, which in turn lessens the need for strong jaw muscles. Food typically passes down into a storage organ called the crop, before moving on to the proventriculus, where the digestive process starts, before passing into the gizzard. Seed-eating birds have a powerful muscular wall to this organ, which grinds up food so that it can be digested more easily. It then continues along the intestinal tract, with nutrients being

FIT FOR PURPOSE The bird's bill serves as a specialist tool, having evolved primarily to obtain food, but also being used for other purposes. These include preening the feathers and helping to build the nest as appropriate, reflecting the lifestyle of the individual species.

GRANIVORE

RAPTOR

SPECIALIST SEED EATER

FISHING

FILTER FEEDER

NECTAR FEEDER

PROBING

INSECTIVORE

NETTING

SURFACE SKIMMING

absorbed mostly in the small intestine. Herbivorous birds have the most complex digestive system, with tubes called caeca connecting to the intestinal tract. Special beneficial microbes are present in these organs, helping the breakdown of plant matter.

THE KIDNEYS

The kidneys of birds produce a highly concentrated urine, and there is no potentially heavy, fluid-filled bladder that would affect their ability to fly. Instead, this semi-solid, whitish material merges with the darker feces at the end of the digestive tract in the cloaca, where the intestinal, renal and reproductive tracts all open, and then exits from the body via the vent.

LUNGS AND HEART

The effort of flying means that birds require high levels of oxygen but, at the same time, their lungs are relatively compact, not moving in the same way during inspiration and expiration as those of mammals. Instead, the lungs connect to a series of air sacs, which act as air reservoirs and also contract like bellows, forcing air through the system. Adjacent air sacs link to the humerus in each wing, which is a pneumatic (hollow) bone. These bones act as further air reservoirs in the bird's body, with the avian skeleton being light overall, again as a way of lessening the energy and oxygen demands of flight.

The avian heart is a four-chambered structure, not dissimilar to that of a mammal, although it works at a much faster rate. Even at rest, the heartbeat of a domestic canary can be about 1,000 beats per minute. This will increase very significantly once the bird is airborne, pumping oxygen-rich blood to the flight muscles.

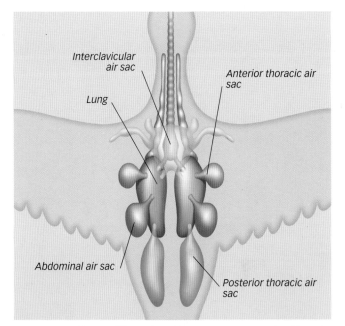

AIR SACS Birds have a different breathing system to mammals. Although they do have lungs, they also have air sacs. Very efficient gaseous uptake in the bird's body is essential, to give sufficient oxygen for the flight muscles.

THE SENSES

Most birds have very keen eyesight, allowing them not just to detect the approach of potential predators and take evasive action, but also to obtain food. The positioning of the eyes gives an indication of a bird's lifestyle. Predatory species such as owls have their eyes at the front of the face, pointing forward. This enables them to locate the position of would-be prey with great accuracy. In contrast, the eyes of game birds such as quail are located on the sides of their face, because here, they afford a much broader field of vision, making it much harder for a predator to creep up on the bird unnoticed. An owl must turn its head to see what is happening on either side.

Most birds do not possess a significant sense of smell, with the notable exception of vultures, in which it enables them to home in on a dead animal, aided by their keen sense of vision. Hearing is also not especially important to birds, although owls are an exception in this case. Hunting at night, their keen hearing helps these birds to detect the high-pitched, ultrasonic calls of rodents, being combined with excellent night-time vision. All birds do have ears, however, as openings covered by feathering on the sides of the head behind the eyes.

Petrels have special valves in their nasal passages. These provide information about the speed of the wind and potential changes in its direction, allowing them to adjust accordingly in flight as they swoop over the oceans, feeding from the surface.

HUNTER AND HUNTED Its forward-facing eyes reveal that the Snowy Owl (*left*) is a predator, able to strike accurately. The Northern Bobwhite's eyes, on the sides of the head, offer better protective all-round vision.

GALLERY OF BIRDS

The following pages reflect the wide diversity of birds found on the North American continent. Some are just summertime visitors, heading back to warmer climes in the late summer or early fall, whereas others are resident throughout the year. Certain species undergo seasonal movement within the continent itself, generally moving to localities where food will be more readily available, and the weather is likely to be less extreme over the winter period. A number have adapted, however, to thrive even under the most severe climatic conditions, remaining within the Arctic Circle throughout the year. Much depends on their diet. Distributions are not static and especially when migrating, birds may be spotted well away from their usual haunts.

NEED TO FEED Dietary needs are one of the strongest influences affecting avian movements. Insectivorous species will face a shortage of food over the course of the northern winter, and so withdraw further south over this period. The same applies to hummingbirds, which depend on flowers for nectar.

GAVIIFORMES
Divers

Members of this Order are often spotted on water, but can disappear very quickly from view, as they dive below the surface in search of food. They are often known collectively as "divers" for this reason. These birds have a very distinctive swimming style, tending to remain low in the water. Loons can also be easily distinguished from other waterfowl by the shape of

their bills, which are relatively long, as well as being narrow and pointed. Depending partly on the species and time of year, they may be observed on both fresh and tidal waters. Their breeding grounds lie in the far north.

Common Loon

FAMILY Gaviidae
SPECIES *Gavia immer*
LENGTH 33 in (84 cm)
HABITAT Lakes/coasts
CLUTCH SIZE 1–3

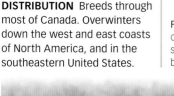

DISTRIBUTION Breeds through most of Canada. Overwinters down the west and east coasts of North America, and in the southeastern United States.

THE BLACK BILL of the Common Loon distinguishes it from the similarly colored but larger Yellow-billed Loon (*Gavia adamsii*), which has a more restricted range in northern Canada. Its plumage over the winter months is much duller overall, with the throat area being white. When hunting fish, Common Loons may dive to depths of 150 ft (46 m).

FAMILY GROUP The chicks can swim soon after hatching, sometimes hitching a ride on the back of one of the adult birds.

Pacific Loon

FAMILY Gaviidae
SPECIES *Gavia pacifica*
LENGTH 26 in (66 cm)
HABITAT Lakes/coastal bays
CLUTCH SIZE 1–3

DISTRIBUTION Breeding range centered to the west of Hudson Bay. Overwinters on the western coast, from the Aleutians and southern Alaska to California.

THERE IS a characteristic purplish-green iridescent area on the throat of these loons when they are in breeding plumage, but it is hard to observe, tending to appear black from some distance away. The throat becomes white during the winter, with a thin brown area, referred to as a chin stripe, being apparent here.

LOW SLUNG The distinctive swimming style of loons means that their bodies are low in the water. They feed mainly on fish. This individual is in breeding plumage.

PODICIPEDIFORMES

Grebes

Grebes are closely tied to areas of fresh water and also coastal areas where they are most likely to be observed over the winter. They will dive underwater in search of food. Perhaps the most obvious distinctive feature of these birds, however, which sets them apart from all other water birds, is their evident lack of tail feathers. Their bill shape varies quite markedly between species, with some having much longer bills than others. Although grebes often tend to be seen either singly or in small groups, larger species may sometimes be observed in much bigger aggregations consisting of hundreds of individuals.

Horned Grebe

FAMILY Podicipedidae
SPECIES *Podiceps auritus*
LENGTH 13½ in (34 cm)
HABITAT Lakes/coastal bays
CLUTCH SIZE 1–7

DISTRIBUTION Breeding range extends from Alaska southeastward across Canada, just across the United States border. Occurs along both coasts in winter, and over much of the southeastern United States.

THE BRIGHT golden plumage on each side of the head gives this species the name of Horned Grebe. During the winter months, however, this feature is not obvious and these grebes are far less colorful. Pairs tend to nest on a stretch of water on their own, but in some areas, pairs may congregate. They rarely come ashore, spending most of their time on water. Even their nest is in the form of a reed raft.

IDENTIFICATION POINTS The Horned Grebe's appearance is unmistakable, especially in breeding plumage. The sexes are identical in plumage.

Pied-billed Grebe

FAMILY Podicipedidae
SPECIES *Podilymbus podiceps*
LENGTH 13½ in (34 cm)
HABITAT Lakes/ponds
CLUTCH SIZE 3–4

DISTRIBUTION Wide summer range from central parts of Canada south down to Kansas and east to Nova Scotia. Resident throughout the rest of the United States.

THIS IS A SMALL, predominantly brown grebe, with a yellowish bill and white plumage under the throat. During the breeding period, birds of both sexes develop a distinctive black band on the bill. These shy grebes retreat to vegetation if they feel under threat, or even dive or submerge so only their head is above the water level. Pied Grebes rarely come on to land.

HABITAT Pied Grebes will move to waters unlikely to freeze over the winter, allowing them to carry on feeding, but they do not congregate on the coast.

PELECANIFORMES

Pelicans, tropicbirds, and their allies

Although the majority of members of this Order are seabirds, often ranging far from land, there are others, such as a number of cormorants, that also can be observed on lakes and other stretches of freshwater. All these birds tend to be either predominantly black or white in color, but they may undergo some dramatic changes in appearance at the start of the breeding season. They have also evolved a range of different yet highly effective fishing techniques. These range from diving down to pursue fish deep underwater through to trawling for them at the surface.

Brown Pelican

FAMILY Pelecanidae
SPECIES *Pelecanus occidentalis*
LENGTH 50 in (127 cm)
HABITAT Open sea
CLUTCH SIZE 2–3

DISTRIBUTION From British Columbia on the Pacific coast, south to Central America. Eastward, extends from New Jersey around the Gulf Coast. Northern range less in winter.

THE BROWN PELICAN, unlike its cousin the American White Pelican, is essentially a marine species. It lives in flocks and constructs a bulky nest of vegetation for its eggs. Adults are a variable shade of grayish-brown, with the back of the neck becoming darker and a yellow patch developing on the throat at the start of the breeding period. The change in Pacific Coast Brown Pelicans is even more marked at this stage, as their bill and pouch lose their gray tones and become red.

Being heavy birds by nature, with large wings measuring 84 inches (213 cm) in span, they appear cumbersome when taking off, particularly from the surface of the sea. Once airborne, however, they can fly quite effortlessly, frequently being seen flying as a flock in single-file formation.

SKYDIVERS Brown Pelicans frequently dive from heights of 30 ft (9 m) into the sea in order to catch fish.

Double-crested Cormorant

FAMILY Phalacrocoracidae

SPECIES *Phalacrocorax auritus*

LENGTH 32 in (81 cm)

HABITAT Coasts/
freshwater

CLUTCH SIZE 2–9

DISTRIBUTION Breeds inland in freshwater areas across the continent, but with resident populations notably around the Gulf coast and south from British Columbia down to Central America.

THE DISTINCTIVE TUFTS of feathers that characterize the Double-crested Cormorant are only apparent during the breeding season. There is a distinctive variance in the separate populations at this stage, with birds from the southeastern race having black crests, whereas this area of plumage is whitish in the case of those occurring elsewhere. These cormorants are the most commonly encountered species in North America, often seen near inland waterways where there are adequate feeding opportunities. They hunt fish, with their hooked bill helping them to seize their quarry more effectively. In flight, these cormorants usually adopt a V-shaped formation, with their necks being held slightly raised. Their wingspan is 52 inches (132 cm).

COMMON SIGHT These birds are often seen close to water, alert to feeding opportunities.

Magnificent Frigatebird

FAMILY Fregatidae

SPECIES *Fregata magnificens*

LENGTH 40 in (102 cm)

HABITAT Open sea

CLUTCH SIZE 1–2

DISTRIBUTION Breeding range includes Florida and the Gulf coast, around to Central America. Also from California southward on the west coast. Resident down to South America.

SOMETIMES DUBBED the pirate of the skies because of the way in which it will harry other birds such as gulls to drop their catches rather than fishing itself, the Magnificent Frigatebird spends much of its time airborne, aided by its 90-inch (229 cm) wingspan. Pairs nest communally, on the ground or in low bushes.

GENDER DIFFERENCES A female is seen here. Males are easily distinguishable by their inflatable orange-red cheek pouches.

CICONIIFORMES

Herons and their allies

Slender in build, long-legged, sometimes secretive and frequently colorful, members of this Order are likely to be encountered in shallow stretches of water. Herons can be seen lurking among reeds and other aquatic vegetation, others such as spoonbills are much easier to observe, living in what can be large flocks. All these birds feed on small aquatic creatures through to fish and frogs. The Florida Everglades is the area in North America where these wading birds are perhaps most numerous. They are concentrated in warmer areas, where their feeding grounds will not be badly affected by ice in winter.

Green Heron

FAMILY Ardeidae
SPECIES *Butorides virescens*
LENGTH 18 in (46 cm)
HABITAT Wooded waterways
CLUTCH SIZE 3–6

DISTRIBUTION Breeds in the eastern United States into Canada, east of the Great Lakes. Resident in Florida along the Gulf Coast. Occurs in the far west.

ADULTS HAVE bluish-gray upperparts with a distinctive greenish suffusion on the back. The wings are dark, but prominently edged with white markings. The sides of the chest have a dull purple hue, with the top of the head being slate-gray while the eyes are orange-yellow. There is a fairly indistinct crest at the back of the crown, which is likely to be held erect if the heron is threatened. At the start of the breeding period, the yellowish legs of the cock bird turn a much brighter orange shade. A pair will nest on their own, constructing a nest of sticks in a well-concealed locality in a tree or bush. Young birds can be recognized by their predominantly brown plumage and will wander off to new territories once they are independent. The adult wingspan is 26 inches (66 cm). Green Herons generally prefer not to wade through water on their relatively short legs when fishing, unlike most other members of the family.

FISHING TECHNIQUE The Green Heron depends on finding a convenient branch from where it can strike at its prey.

Great Blue Heron

FAMILY Ardeidae
SPECIES *Ardea herodias*
LENGTH 46 in (117 cm)
HABITAT Wetland
CLUTCH SIZE 3–7

DISTRIBUTION Throughout the United States into Canada during the summer; south of the Great Lakes in the east; in the west, resident up to Alaska.

AS THEIR NAME suggests, most Great Blue Herons are bluish in color, with a black stripe on each side of the head, extending back through the eyes, and on the shoulder area. White areas are restricted to the head and underparts, with white plumes evident over the neck and wings. In Florida, however, there is a totally white form, which used to be regarded as a separate species, while another variant, called Wurdemann's Heron, is characterized by its white head. These herons are solitary outside the breeding period, sometimes flying up to 15 miles (24 km) for food. They breed colonially, on cliffs or in trees or bushes, and occasionally, there may be hundreds nesting together.

BIG IMPACT The Great Blue is the largest heron in North America, having a wingspan of 72 inches (183 cm), and also has the widest distribution.

ANSERIFORMES

Waterfowl and screamers

The ducks, geese, and swans comprise by far the largest of the two families that make up this Order, with approximately 159 species recognized worldwide. There are just three species of screamers, which are confined to parts of South America. The members of the Anatidae are known collectively as waterfowl, reflecting the fact that they live in the vicinity of water. Chicks will start to swim very soon after hatching.

Brant Goose

FAMILY Anatidae
SPECIES *Branta bernicla*
LENGTH 25 in (64 cm)
HABITAT Bays/marshland
CLUTCH SIZE 1–7

DISTRIBUTION Alaska into the far north, mainly west of Hudson Bay. Winter range includes the Aleutian Islands, plus the west and northeastern coasts of the United States.

THESE GEESE have a circumpolar distribution, occurring in northern Europe and Asia as well as North America. They are sometimes known as Brent Geese. The eastern American subspecies (*Branta bernicla hrota*) has a white abdomen, whereas that of the western race (*B. b. nigricans*) is dark.

MARKINGS Brant Geese display a variable white band on the side of the neck; the head and neck are dark.

Canada Goose

FAMILY Anatidae
SPECIES *Branta canadensis*
LENGTH 45 in (114 cm)
HABITAT Fields/grassland
CLUTCH SIZE 2–12

DISTRIBUTION Summer range extends right up to parts of the continent's northern coastline. Resident down the west coast and generally across an area south of the Great Lakes.

CANADA GEESE can be found over virtually the entire North American continent, at different times of the year. Flocks migrate in a distinctive V-shaped formation. They are very adaptable, increasingly being seen in city parks and on golf courses. Flocks can cause considerable damage in fields, by feeding on growing cereal crops. Pairs will construct a large nest using vegetation, lining it with down feathers.

NESTING Canada Geese are especially protective in the vicinity of their nest, hissing menacingly if disturbed. They breed on the ground near water, and the female incubates alone, with the goslings hatching after about 25 days.

Green-winged Teal

FAMILY Anatidae

SPECIES *Anas crecca*

LENGTH 14½ in (37 cm)

HABITAT Marshland

CLUTCH SIZE 10–12

DISTRIBUTION Widely distributed over much of North America, breeding in the northern half of the continent and overwintering across the entire south, down into Mexico.

THE GREEN AREA on the wings of these teal is present in both sexes, but only the drake has the broad, dark green stripe extending down the neck from behind the eye on each side of the face. Ducks in contrast are predominantly brown in color. Green-winged Teal are very social by nature, sometimes forming large flocks consisting of hundreds of birds during the winter period. Such groups look spectacular when in flight. When feeding, these waterfowl forage in a typical dabbling duck fashion, upending their bodies to feed underwater.

SMALL BUT COLORFUL This species—the drake seen here in breeding plumage—is the smallest of the dabbling ducks in North America.

Blue-winged Teal

FAMILY Anatidae

SPECIES *Anas discors*

LENGTH 15½ in (39 cm)

HABITAT Lakes/marshland

CLUTCH SIZE 6–15

DISTRIBUTION Widely distributed summer visitor across much of the United States into southern Canada. Generally overwinters in northern South America.

BOTH SEXES DISPLAY the pale blue wing patch that is a feature of this species. Ducks and drakes out of breeding colors are a mottled shade of grayish-brown, with the young being a paler shade of brown with yellow legs. They sometimes occur in very small stretches of water, and may be seen in groups in marshland too.

FEEDING Blue-winged Teal tend not to tip up their bodies like other dabbling ducks when feeding, but simply extend their necks below the surface.

Mallard

FAMILY Anatidae

SPECIES *Anas platyrhynchos*

LENGTH 23 in (58 cm)

HABITAT Freshwater/
marshland

CLUTCH SIZE 5–14

DISTRIBUTION Found through Alaska in the summer eastward to Newfoundland. Resident on the western seaboard and across most of the United States.

MALLARDS ARE very conspicuous waterfowl, frequently seen in city parks where there are ponds, as well as on rivers and even in coastal marshes. Drakes have a dark green head and brown chest, and pale flanks, with ducks having a mottled appearance. There are blue patches evident across the wings. Young Mallards resemble adult females, but have dull olive rather than black-marked orange bills. Courting drakes can be very persistent, with a number chasing a single female, and occasionally even exhausting her so that she drowns.

A PAIR OF MALLARDS This species is actually the original ancestor of the majority of today's domesticated breeds of duck.

Wood Duck

FAMILY Anatidae

SPECIES *Aix sponsa*

LENGTH 18½ in (47 cm)

HABITAT Woodland with water

CLUTCH SIZE 8–14

DISTRIBUTION Found in the summer throughout southern Canada and eastern half of the United States, being resident in southern areas here. Resident too along the west coast.

THESE DUCKS ARE UNUSUAL because they roost and breed as high as 50 ft (15 m) off the ground, in a suitable hollow tree. The young ducklings, unable to fly at first, simply tumble down to the ground from the nest site soon after hatching. Their mother watches over them once they take to the water, and the family group will typically remain together for almost two months.

SPECTACULAR The drake, seen here on the right, is one of the most colorful of North America's waterfowl. This species is also known as the Carolina Duck.

Common Eider

FAMILY Anatidae

SPECIES *Somateria mollissima*

LENGTH 24 in (61 cm)

HABITAT Tundra ponds/
coastal bays

CLUTCH SIZE 4–7

DISTRIBUTION Breeds from southern Alaska around the northern coast and Greenland, partly resident here and down the northeastern coast. Also overwinters off Alaska and in Hudson Bay.

COMMON EIDER DUCKS BREED on tundra ponds formed in the summer by the thawing of ice in the upper layers of the ground. They then move to coastal areas to overwinter, feeding on marine invertebrates such as crustaceans and starfish, as well as small fish.

BREEDING PLUMAGE This male Common Eider shows the species' distinctive head profile. The female is brown.

Ring-necked Duck

FAMILY Anatidae

SPECIES *Aythya collaris*

LENGTH 17 in (43 cm)

HABITAT Lakes/ponds/
marshland

CLUTCH SIZE 6–14

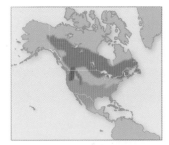

DISTRIBUTION Summer range from southern Alaska to Nova Scotia, around the Great Lakes and Colorado in the west. Winters down both coasts and across the southern United States.

UNLIKE MANY WATERFOWL, the Ring-necked Duck tends to be quite solitary by nature, and does not occur in large flocks. It tends to frequent stretches of freshwater, but may sometimes be encountered in coastal marshes. A gray wing stripe helps to identify these waterfowl in flight.

BREEDING COLORS This drake clearly displays the whitish stripes evident across the bill.

Lesser Scaup

FAMILY Anatidae
SPECIES *Aythya affinis*
LENGTH 16½ in (42 cm)
HABITAT Ponds/coastal bays
CLUTCH SIZE 9–12

DISTRIBUTION Breeds from Alaska eastward, generally overwintering across the entire United States south of the Great Lakes, down into Central America and the Caribbean, but resident further west.

THIS SPECIES RANGES over a much greater area than its cousin the Greater Scaup, not being confined to coastal areas over the winter. They appear very similar, but aside from being smaller, the Lesser Scaup also has a reduced area of white plumage across each wing.

COLORATION The drake is brownish overall in nonbreeding plumage.

Redhead

FAMILY Anatidae
SPECIES *Aythya americana*
LENGTH 19 in (48 cm)
HABITAT Lakes/marshland
CLUTCH SIZE 7–12

DISTRIBUTION Isolated breeding population in Alaska, and southern Yukon Territory down to west of the Great Lakes. Overwinters in southern United States and Central America.

ALTHOUGH ITS OVERALL COLORATION is not dissimilar to that of the Canvasback, the Redhead drake can be identified in breeding plumage by even chestnut-red coloration over the entire head, and its yellow rather than red eyes. The duck in contrast is brown, with the feathering on the crown being of a darker shade. The Redhead's bill is gray with a black tip, providing a further point of distinction between these species.

NESTING Redheads nest in reed beds, constructing a nest here lined with soft down. Unusually, females may lay eggs in other neighboring nests as well.

Common Goldeneye

FAMILY Anatidae

SPECIES *Bucephala clangula*

LENGTH 18½ in (47 cm)

HABITAT Lakes/rivers

CLUTCH SIZE 6–15

DISTRIBUTION Breeding range extends through much of Canada, from Alaska to Newfoundland. Overwinters through the majority of the United States, and resident especially around the Great Lakes.

THESE WATERFOWL have been nicknamed "whistler," thanks to the sound of their wings when they are flying. Drakes can be recognized by the large white circular areas on each side of the face, between their golden-colored eyes and their bill. Ducks have a brown head and gray body.

NESTING Common Goldeneyes breed in areas of coniferous forests, nesting in tree holes.

Barrow's Goldeneye

FAMILY Anatidae

SPECIES *Bucephala islandica*

LENGTH 18 in (46 cm)

HABITAT Lakes/rivers

CLUTCH SIZE 9–10

DISTRIBUTION Western population breeds from Alaska to the Northwest Territory, and to British Columbia. Eastern range centered on Newfoundland and Maine.

THESE DIVING DUCKS prefer colder northern waters, not venturing as far south as the Common Goldeneye. Pairs nest in tree cavities. When their young hatch, after about 32 days, they plummet to the ground, which can represent a drop of 50 ft (15 m) or more, and head to water with their mother. It is likely to be two months before they can fly. There are two separate breeding populations in North America: A larger, western one, and a smaller, eastern-based one.

SPECIES IDENTIFICATION
The Barrow's Goldeneye drake (*left*) can be separated from the Common Goldeneye by the fact that is has a crescent-shaped area of white plumage on the face.

Ruddy Duck

FAMILY Anatidae

SPECIES *Oxyura jamaicensis*

LENGTH 15 in (38 cm)

HABITAT Woodland lakes/
rivers

CLUTCH SIZE 5–17

DISTRIBUTION Breeds mainly in western and central parts up to Alaska, and near the Great Lakes. Resident in the southwest, and winter range extends through the south.

THESE SMALL DIVING DUCKS often congregate in large flocks. They can be distinguished easily by their stiff tail feathers, which may be carried vertically. Even young ducklings will dive in search of food, rather than dabbling at the surface, when they first take to the water.

GENDER DIFFERENCES
The cock (*left*) is in breeding plumage. These ducks may be seen in coastal bays in winter.

Common Merganser

FAMILY Anatidae

SPECIES *Mergus merganser*

LENGTH 25 in (64 cm)

HABITAT Woodland lakes/
rivers

CLUTCH SIZE 6–12

DISTRIBUTION Summer breeding range extends right across North America, from Alaska to Newfoundland. Overwinters in the south.

THE LARGE SIZE of these mergansers aids their identification. They also display the narrow bills that are characteristic of this group of ducks. As in other species, the bill is serrated along its upper edge, and this has led to mergansers being referred to as sawbills. This is believed to help them to grab slippery prey such as frogs, which would otherwise be more likely to slip from their grasp. The duck can be recognized by the rusty-red plumage on her head, and white throat and gray body.

MALE PLUMAGE
The drake of this species has a white body, contrasting with the dark green head, and the black plumage on the back.

FALCONIFORMES   Birds of prey

Although some members of this Order are large in size, others are surprisingly small, reflecting the adaptability of the group as a whole. All members are predatory birds, but they may not be active hunters. A number of species, notably vultures, scavenge on carcasses, while others will avail themselves of carrion when it is available. All species have a hooked bill, and powerful feet, equipped with curved nails often described as talons. These two features enable them to catch and hold their prey more effectively. As they are at the top of the food chain, birds of prey are generally not very numerous.

Turkey Vulture

FAMILY Cathartidae
SPECIES *Cathartes aura*
LENGTH 27 in (69 cm)
HABITAT Open country
CLUTCH SIZE 1–3

DISTRIBUTION Summer visitor from southern Canada across the United States, resident across the southeastern United States.

IN COMMON WITH other vultures, the Turkey Vulture is essentially bald on its head. This is thought to allow these birds to feed on the carcasses of large animals without fear of their plumage becoming contaminated and matted by blood. The red coloration of the skin here is reminiscent of the appearance of a Wild Turkey, explaining this vulture's common name. The keen sense of smell of these birds of prey helps them locate dead animals. They spend much of the day gliding with their wings outstretched on warm currents of air called thermals, which allow them to stay airborne with minimum effort. When breeding, the hen will lay on the ground, often in a cave on a cliff face, or sometimes even in a deserted building. It will take about 40 days for the eggs to hatch.

LARGE SPREAD The wingspan of these vultures can exceed 67 inches (170 cm) from the tip of one wing to the other.

Red-tailed Hawk

FAMILY Accipitridae

SPECIES *Buteo jamaicensis*

LENGTH 22 in (56 cm)

HABITAT Open country/ woodland

CLUTCH SIZE 1–4

DISTRIBUTION Breeds from central Alaska across Canada to southern Newfoundland, to northern-central United States. Resident through United States.

THE RED-TAILED HAWK is one of the most widely distributed and commonly seen North American hawks, ranging over a wide area of the continent, particularly in summer. They frequent areas of open country where there are stands of trees nearby, which can be utilized for roosting and breeding purposes. These hawks prove very patient hunters, perching in the open. Rodents feature prominently in their diet. In flight, their red tail feathers are less evident, because the undersides tend to be whitish. The underparts of the body are whitish too, with darker streaking. Pairs frequently choose to nest at a considerable height, perhaps 70 ft (21 m) or more off the ground. They build a large structure using twigs and other vegetation, either on a cliff or in a mature tree, for their eggs.

PLUMAGE The coloration of the Red-tailed Hawk can vary markedly, with some individuals being a much darker shade of brown than others. Their tail color may vary too. Their wings measure 50 inches (127 cm) across when spread.

Swainson's Hawk

FAMILY Accipitridae
SPECIES *Buteo swainsoni*
LENGTH 21 in (53 cm)
HABITAT Open grassland
CLUTCH SIZE 2–4

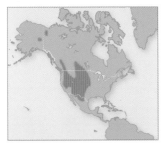

DISTRIBUTION Summertime visitor in southwestern Canada southward down through the United States to Mexico. Overwinters in South America.

THESE HAWKS have adapted to changes in the landscape, forming a remarkable relationship with farmers in some areas. They follow harvesting machinery in the fields, swooping down on rodents that are flushed from the vegetation. Swainson's Hawks breed in the United States each year, with pairs often returning to the same site and repairing their nest in the spring. Incubation, which is shared by both parents, lasts for a month. In flight, these hawks have a slim profile, with a small head. Their wings span 52 inches (132 cm) and are relatively narrow in shape.

VARIETY The coloration of Swainson's Hawk is very variable, with some birds being much darker on their underparts than others.

Osprey

FAMILY Panionidae
SPECIES *Pandion haliaetus*
LENGTH 23 in (58 cm)
HABITAT Coasts/lakes
CLUTCH SIZE 2–4

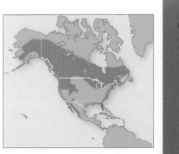

DISTRIBUTION Summer visitor across much of Canada, also seen in the western United States and the southeast; resident here along the coast and in Florida.

THESE HIGHLY SPECIALIZED fish hawks are very strong and agile, being able to catch and lift their quarry from the surface of the water. Their upperparts are dark brown, with the dark eye stripes serving to highlight the yellow coloration of the eyes.

IDENTIFICATION The Osprey's head and underparts are predominantly white. These hawks prefer to feed off the ground, as here. In this picture, the impressive wings, spanning 63 inches (160 cm), are clearly visible.

Bald Eagle

FAMILY Accipitridae

SPECIES *Haliaeetus leucocephalus*

LENGTH 31 in (79 cm)

HABITAT Coasts/inland waters

CLUTCH SIZE 1–3

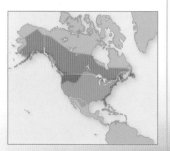

DISTRIBUTION Ranges across Canada in the summer; resident along the west and eastern coasts of North America. Resident in the central and western United States, overwintering across the country.

THERE IS NO MISTAKING the identity of the Bald Eagle. Its population had fallen dramatically by the 1970s, because of the build-up of toxic chemicals in its food, which adversely affected its breeding. Since legislation banned the most damaging of such chemicals, the numbers of Bald Eagles have grown again, and they can be seen across most of the continent. They will hunt fish themselves, and also rob Ospreys of their catches. Along the shoreland, these eagles will also scavenge on the carcasses of bigger sea mammals washed up here. Larger numbers may congregate in areas where food is readily available. Pairs nest in trees, often as high as 150 ft (46 m) off the ground, with the young eagles remaining here until they are about 10 weeks old.

ICONIC IMAGE A very powerful yellowish bill, a white head plus a brown body and white tail, and a massive wingspan of 80 inches (203 cm), are characteristics of the Bald Eagle.

Gyrfalcon

FAMILY Falconidae
SPECIES *Falco rusticolus*
LENGTH 22 in (56 cm)
HABITAT Tundra/cliffs
CLUTCH SIZE 3–8

DISTRIBUTION Resident across the far north of the continent, including southern Greenland, and ranges further south across Canada in winter. Summer visitor to northern Greenland.

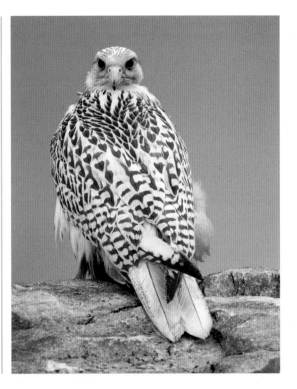

THIS FALCON is restricted to the far north, with its whitish plumage helping to provide some camouflage in the snowy landscape there. Their underparts are usually much lighter in color than their upperparts. They have the ability to fly quickly, thanks to their powerful wings measuring 47 inches (119 cm) in span, but also with relatively little effort. Gyrfalcons hunt ptarmigans and also rodents, such as lemmings. When nesting, a pair may utilize a ledge on a cliff face for this purpose. The incubation period lasts approximately a month and it will be a further seven weeks before the young falcons fledge.

FEMALE GYRFALCON Individual Gyrfalcons differ quite widely in appearance, with some being much whiter than others. They have long tail feathers, as seen here.

American Kestrel

FAMILY Falconidae
SPECIES *Falco sparverius*
LENGTH 10½ in (27 cm)
HABITAT Open country/cities
CLUTCH SIZE 3–6

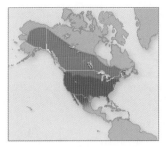

DISTRIBUTION Occurs over most of the continent; summer visitor to Canada and northern-central United States, but resident elsewhere in the United States, especially in Texas where it overwinters.

THIS IS THE SMALLEST falcon occurring within North America, and also one of the most common, being found both in rural and city environments, often being seen in the vicinity of parks. Like other falcons, the American Kestrel has keen eyesight, enabling it to spot potential prey on the ground below as it hovers overhead. Sometimes, it may be seen resting on a telephone wire, but it will dive down if a hunting opportunity presents itself. Rodents and invertebrates are the main item in the diet of these kestrels, but they may also take small birds, too.

PAIR OF AMERICAN KESTRELS The more colorful cock bird is evident here on the right, with blue-gray wings. The species' wingspan is 23 inches (58 cm).

GALLIFORMES

Pheasants, partridges, and grouse

These species are generally ground-dwellers, well-adapted to move on foot, although they can fly if danger threatens. Their flight tends to be quite clumsy, however, and they will glide down to another suitable area of cover relatively nearby in most cases. Cock birds can generally be distinguished by their brighter plumage. In some species, polygamy occurs, with a male being surrounded by a group of hens, while in other cases, communal displays permit the hens to choose their own mates. Young birds are able to follow their parents from the point of hatching, although they cannot fly at this stage.

Spruce Grouse

FAMILY Tetraonidae

SPECIES *Dendragapus canadensis*

LENGTH 16 in (41 cm)

HABITAT Coniferous forest

CLUTCH SIZE 6–12

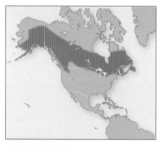

DISTRIBUTION Resident through much of Alaska and Canada, right across to Newfoundland. Extends to eastern Oregon, also just south of the Great Lakes, and the northeastern United States.

DIET Spruce Grouse feed largely on conifer needles, particularly in the winter when other food is scarce.

THESE GROUSE LIVE individually in the forests that they inhabit, coming together only briefly for mating, when the male displays by fanning his tail, calling, and strutting to attract a would-be mate. The sexes are easy to distinguish throughout the year, with the cock bird being slate-gray on the back with paler barring on the edges of the feathers, while hens are brown rather than gray here. The female will construct a simple nest in undergrowth, using grass to line a hollow. Her mottled plumage then helps to conceal her presence when she is incubating the eggs. The young grouse are able to follow her immediately after hatching, but it will be a while before they can fly.

Wild Turkey

FAMILY Meleagrididae
SPECIES *Meleagris gallopavo*
LENGTH 46 in (117 cm)
HABITAT Oak woodland
CLUTCH SIZE 8–16

DISTRIBUTION Occurs largely within the United States, particularly in the east in suitable habitat, although absent from northern Minnesota, but ranges up to southern Manitoba in Canada.

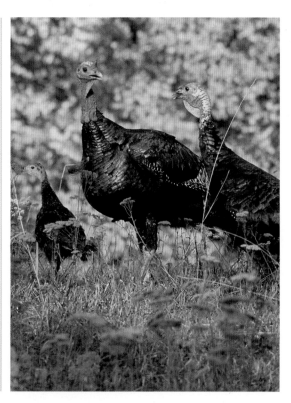

THIS SPECIES is the ancestor of the domesticated turkey, and is a bird of shady woodland, favoring areas where there are oaks, whose acorns provide a source of food over the winter months. Males are significantly larger in size, and fan their tail feathers as part of their display. There are regional variations, with birds from eastern areas having chestnut tipping to these feathers, whereas those from the west have white tips instead. The head is red and bluish, while the plumage is iridescent in part. Hens have duller feathering and they also lack the long breast tuft of feathers associated with the male turkey, or stag.

FLIGHT Wild Turkeys are able to fly well and will roost in trees at night. Sadly, hunting pressure means this species is now quite scarce.

Northern Bobwhite

FAMILY Odontophoridae
SPECIES *Colinus virginianus*
LENGTH 9¼ in (24 cm)
HABITAT Woodland
CLUTCH SIZE 10–15

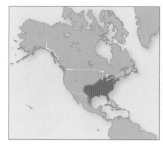

DISTRIBUTION Widely distributed through eastern-central parts, south of the Great Lakes. Isolated populations in Washington, as well as on the Idaho-Oregon border and in Arizona.

NORTHERN BOBWHITES live on the ground, in flocks numbering as many as 30 birds, which are often described as coveys. These quails feed on seeds and insects. During the spring, pairs nest on their own, choosing a well-concealed locality where the hen will lay her eggs in a small depression on the ground. Both sexes incubate the eggs, and it takes about three weeks for hatching to occur. The young chicks can then follow their parents, although they will not be able to fly at this stage.

GENDER DIFFERENCES
The cock bird (*left*) can be identified by its black rather than gray eye stripe, and white areas on the face.

GRUIFORMES

Coots and cranes

The members of this Order found in North America vary significantly in size, from cranes down to coots, but generally they are linked with an aquatic environment. This can vary from saltwater areas through to freshwater, with some species being quite adaptable in this regard.

They can be migratory too, as in the case of cranes. Many of these species are often shy birds by nature, and not easy to observe. Most of these birds are dull colored.

American Coot

FAMILY Rallidae
SPECIES *Fulica americana*
LENGTH 15½ in (39 cm)
HABITAT Marshland
CLUTCH SIZE 8–20

DISTRIBUTION Summer visitor north to Yukon Territory, and eastward to southern Quebec. Resident in western and central parts of the United States; winter migrant in the east.

URBAN These coots are often resident in city parks where there is a pond nearby. They may forage for invertebrates on the grass in these surroundings.

THE BLACK PLUMAGE of the American coot contrasts with its ivory-colored forehead shield and similarly colored bill. There is a small reddish area at the top of the shield, and a dark band encircling the bill near its tip. The most remarkable feature of these birds is hidden, however, when they are in the water. They have flattened bluish lobed extensions on their toes, which serve as primitive webbing, helping them to swim. American Coots have a particularly distinctive style of swimming, nodding their heads forward as they move. They can dive if necessary in search of food, or feed at the surface.

Common Moorhen

FAMILY Rallidae
SPECIES *Gallinula chloropus*
LENGTH 14 in (36 cm)
HABITAT Freshwater
CLUTCH SIZE 8–12

DISTRIBUTION Breeds mainly in central-eastern parts of the United States, up to Maine. Resident from North Carolina down through Texas and along the Mexican border.

THESE WATER BIRDS are dark in color, but can easily be identified by the red shield on the forehead, which merges into the bill. This in turn becomes yellow at its tip. Common Moorhens are very adaptable birds, and can be encountered in a wide range of habitats from ponds and freshwater marshes to rivers. They are quite shy, and may be seen skulking along the edge of the pond, disappearing into reeds here at any hint of a threat. Their long toes assist them in walking across aquatic vegetation.

APPEARANCE Common Moorhens have a white area on the flanks. Although often seen in shallow water, these birds can swim well.

Sandhill Crane

FAMILY Gruidae
SPECIES *Grus canadensis*
LENGTH 42 in (107 cm)
HABITAT Tundra/grassland
CLUTCH SIZE 2

DISTRIBUTION Main summer breeding range extends from Alaska to the eastern coast of Hudson Bay, south and southeast, to northern California and Iowa. Overwinters in southern states.

SANDHILL CRANES vary in size through their range, with those from southern areas being larger than those found in the north. Their appearance is unmistakable, on grounds of their coloration as well as their stature. The top of the head, extending up and around the eyes from the base of the bill, is reddish, with the remainder of their plumage being grayish, with a variable brownish hue apparent, particularly over the wings, and a paler, whitish area beneath the throat. In their Arctic breeding grounds, a pair will build a large mound of vegetation as their nest. Once the young cranes hatch, it will be 10 weeks before they can fly.

FEEDING HABITS These cranes are omnivorous, consuming small animals, fish, and plant matter too. They have a large wingspan of between 73 and 90 inches (185–229 cm)

CHARADRIIFORMES

Waders, gulls, and their allies

The Charadriiformes are a diverse group of birds, divided into 19 families, whose representatives are often seen either in coastal areas or in grasslands. Members of this Order include typical shorebirds, observed wandering along the coast line, following tidal movements and congregating on mud flats. They may then move inland to grassland areas during the breeding season. Members of other families, such as the gulls, can be encountered some distance out at sea, and also inland, while others like auks spend most of their lives on the world's oceans.

Semipalmated Plover

FAMILY Charadriidae
SPECIES *Charadrius semipalmatus*
LENGTH 7½ in (19 cm)
HABITAT Beaches/lakes
CLUTCH SIZE 4

DISTRIBUTION Summer visitor to the far north, where it is present throughout Alaska, north to Baffin Island, and along Hudson Bay.

SEMIPALMATED PLOVERS breed in the summer in the far north, taking advantage of the temporary pools caused by the meltwater on the tundra where small insects proliferate. For the remainder of the year, they are likely to be seen in coastal areas, on beaches and tidal flats in estuaries, as they overwinter on the east and west United States' coasts. They have a white collar with a black bib, and a white face and underparts. The wings are brownish in color. There is a thin whitish stripe above the eyes and the bill.

DISTINCTIVE FEATURES The tip of the bill is blackish, with a yellowish-orange area encircling its base. The legs are also yellowish-orange.

Killdeer

FAMILY Charadriidae
SPECIES *Charadrius vociferus*
LENGTH 10½ in (27 cm)
HABITAT Field and shorelines
CLUTCH SIZE 4

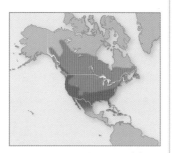

DISTRIBUTION Summer visitor to southern Alaska and northwest Canada, and to Newfoundland in the east. Resident up both coasts and across the southern United States.

THESE PLOVERS can be observed in habitats ranging from grassland to the shores of lakes. Killdeer live in flocks, and feed on a variety of invertebrates, ranging from snails to worms. Their characteristic reddish-orange rump will only be evident when the birds are in flight. They nest on open ground, and both adults take turns to incubate the eggs.

DISTINCTIVE The double chest band of the Killdeer is unique to this species, making identification easy.

Greater Yellowlegs

FAMILY Scolopacidae
SPECIES *Tringa melanoleuca*
LENGTH 14 in (36 cm)
HABITAT Shallow wetland
CLUTCH SIZE 3–4

DISTRIBUTION Breeding range extends right across North America, south of Hudson Bay and up to Newfoundland. Overwinters from Washington to Mexico, and along America's east coast.

SPECKLED BLACK-AND-WHITE plumage over back and wings, paler underparts, and yellow legs help to identify these waders. They breed over a wide area in Canada, but their wintering grounds are more restricted. Greater Yellowlegs form mixed flocks with other waders, hunting for invertebrates and small fish.

IDENTIFICATION A slightly upturned bill, long neck, mottled back, and yellow legs all aid identification.

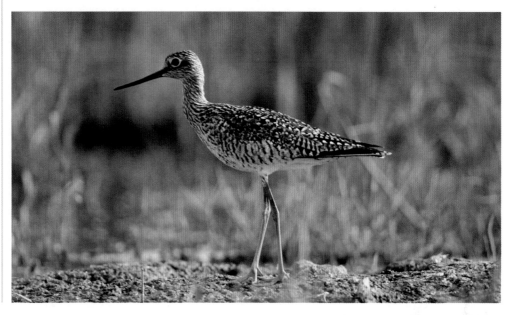

Spotted Sandpiper

FAMILY Scolopacidae
SPECIES *Actitis macularia*
LENGTH 7½ in (19 cm)
HABITAT Streams/marshland
CLUTCH SIZE 3–4

DISTRIBUTION Breeds from Alaska to Texas, but absent from here to the Carolinas southward. Resident down the west coast. Overwinters in the southern United States.

THE SPOTTED SANDPIPER has an extensive breeding area in North America, being seen in a variety of habitats close to water, in coastal areas as well as inland. It moves with a very distinctive bobbing gait, and flies in quite a stiff way, revealing the white area in each wing. The back is olive-brown, with this coloration extending down the sides of the neck. The eggs are laid in a scrape near water, and it appears that often the cock bird incubates for much of the time on his own.

DISTINCTIVE The Spotted Sandpiper is easily identified during the breeding season, with circular black markings evident on its otherwise white underparts.

Least Sandpiper

FAMILY Scolopacidae
SPECIES *Calidris minutilla*
LENGTH 6 in (15 cm)
HABITAT Rivers/marshland
CLUTCH SIZE 4

DISTRIBUTION Summer range extends over the far north, from Alaska across to Newfoundland. Overwinters down the United States' east and west coast, and across the southern states.

THESE SMALL sandpipers are commonly seen inland in parts of North America when they are migrating. Their appearance in the summer period is rather similar to that of other *Calidris* sandpipers, and these birds may be seen as part of mixed flocks feeding together, making accurate identification harder. Their legs are yellowish, however, unlike those of the Western Sandpiper.

SEASONAL CHANGE This Least Sandpiper is in summer plumage. Their upperparts become gray after the breeding period, with their underparts being completely white. Young birds are a more rufous gray in color.

Rock Sandpiper

FAMILY Scolopacidae
SPECIES *Calidris ptilocnemis*
LENGTH 9 in (23 cm)
HABITAT Tundra/rocky shores
CLUTCH SIZE 4

DISTRIBUTION Summer breeding range is on the west coast of Alaska and islands here. Overwinters along the coast from southern Alaska down to northern California.

AS ITS NAME SUGGESTS, this particular sandpiper favors rocky areas of coastline where it overwinters. Similar in size and coloration to the Purple Sandpiper, these birds can be distinguished by the presence of a dark gray area of plumage on the lower breast. The bill is quite long and black in color, curving slightly downward along its length. The legs and feet are yellowish-green. On their breeding grounds, pairs utilize a simple nest, lined with plant matter. The young birds are able to run around as soon as they hatch, covered in downy feathering.

DISTINGUISHING FEATURE When these sandpipers take to the air, it is usually possible to see the white stripe running across each wing.

Long-billed Dowitcher

FAMILY Scolopacidae

SPECIES *Limnodromus scolopaceus*

LENGTH 11½ in (29 cm)

HABITAT Tundra/mudflats

CLUTCH SIZE 4

DISTRIBUTION Summer range restricted to the far northwest, primarily in Alaska. In winter, occurs on both the Atlantic and Pacific United States' coasts, and across the southern states.

CONTRARY TO THEIR NAMES, the bill length in the case of cock birds of this species and that of the Short-billed Dowitcher are almost identical. Where there is an evident variance, however, it is in the case of hens. After leaving their breeding grounds, Long-billed Dowitchers will head to freshwater localities rather than to the coast, unlike their Short-billed relative. They use their long bill to probe for food such as snails and other invertebrates in environments that may vary from shallow pools to marshland. The eggs of the Long-billed Dowitcher tend to blend in against the area of surrounding grass where they are laid, being green with dark spots. The eggs will be incubated by both parents and should hatch after about three weeks.

PLUMAGE When in breeding condition, the Long-billed Dowitcher cock bird has chestnut-orange on the neck, and orange underparts. The back is overlaid with rufous plumage.

Wilson's Snipe

FAMILY Scolopacidae

SPECIES *Gallinago delicata*

LENGTH 10½ in (27 cm)

HABITAT Marshland/wet fields

CLUTCH SIZE 4

DISTRIBUTION Ranges up to Alaska and to Newfoundland in the summer. Resident in western United States especially, and also overwinters widely across the southern United States.

THESE BIRDS ARE hard to observe, because of their secretive natures, and their mottled coloration helps them to blend into the background in their marshy habitat. When flushed from cover, they fly in a very distinctive zig-zag pattern. Wilson's Snipe uses its long bill to catch invertebrates of various types, probing in mud for worms. The hen lays on the ground, lining the scrape with grasses as a cushion for her eggs. The incubation period lasts for approximately 20 days, and the young will be independent after a similar interval.

WARY BEHAVIOR It is rare to spot a Wilson's Snipe out in the open. These birds are very alert to any hint of danger.

Herring Gull

FAMILY Laridae
SPECIES *Larus argentatus*
LENGTH 25 in (64 cm)
HABITAT Coasts/lakes
CLUTCH SIZE 2–3

DISTRIBUTION Breeds across a broad area of northern North America. Resident in northeastern parts. Winters through the southeast and in the west.

ADULTS OF THIS SPECIES can be identified by their bill color, which is yellowish with a prominent red spot on the lower mandible, near its tip. The head, neck, and underparts are white, and the wings gray. The flight feathers are black, with white spots at their tips. In winter plumage, the neck is streaked with brown, and the red on the bill becomes less distinctive. Herring Gulls will feed on fish, but they are effectively scavengers, eating anything edible. This has seen them move further inland, away from the coast, often into cities where they may nest on the roofs of tall buildings. Pairs have very protective parental instincts, dive-bombing people who venture too close to the nest or chicks after they have fledged.

COLORATION This is a young Herring Gull, as shown by its mottled brown plumage and dark bill. As an adult, its wingspan will reach 57 inches (145 cm).

Laughing Gull

FAMILY Laridae
SPECIES *Larus atricilla*
LENGTH 16½ in (42 cm)
HABITAT Sea/marshland
CLUTCH SIZE 3–4

DISTRIBUTION Resident from North Carolina along the Gulf Coast, and inland Florida in winter. In summer may range up to Nova Scotia.

THE SOUND OF the calls of this gull helps to explain its common name—they resemble the sound of someone laughing. It is primarily found along the coast, but moves further inland, typically to areas of salt marsh, when nesting. These birds breed here in colonies. The young gulls should hatch after a period of about three weeks, but it will take three years for them to acquire adult coloring and a wingspan of 40 inches (102 cm). During the winter, Laughing Gulls have largely white heads, with some darker speckling evident here.

IDENTIFICATION A Laughing Gull in summer plumage, as reflected by the black plumage on the head. The sexes are identical in appearance.

Mew Gull

FAMILY Laridae
SPECIES *Larus canus*
LENGTH 16 in (41 cm)
HABITAT Coasts/lakes
CLUTCH SIZE 2–3

DISTRIBUTION From Alaska to the Northwest Territories and northern Manitoba, and south on the west coast. Winter visitor here from Washington to California.

A NARROW YELLOW BILL and yellow legs help to distinguish the Mew Gull. The plumage over the back and wings is grayish, with the underparts being white. Over the winter period, the white area on the head and neck has a brownish suffusion. Mew Gulls nest in colonies, sometimes alongside other species of gull in their northern breeding range. They then overwinter along the coast. This species feeds on invertebrates such as worms and molluscs, rather than scavenging. Young birds can be recognized by their brown, mottled appearance, and it takes three years for them to acquire full adult plumage. Their eventual wingspan will be 43 inches (109 cm). Juveniles lack the white spots at the tips of the flight feathers, and have brown spotting on their underparts.

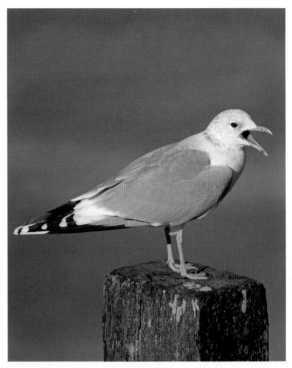

DISTINCTIVE SOUND The call of the Mew Gull has been likened to the miaowing sound made by a cat! They also have a more guttural call note.

Ring-billed Gull

FAMILY Laridae
SPECIES *Larus delawarensis*
LENGTH 17½ in (44 cm)
HABITAT Coasts/inland waters
CLUTCH SIZE 3

DISTRIBUTION Central Canada east to Newfoundland in summer. Resident in the north-western United States and the Great Lakes. Overwinters across much of the south.

THE MOST DISTINCTIVE feature of this gull is the dark tip around its bill, which is otherwise yellow in color. The legs too are yellow, and its basic coloration corresponds to that of other species. There is a narrow red area of bare skin encircling the eyes. Although young birds fledge with blackish bills, the distinctive dark tip will be apparent by their first winter. They will grow to have a wingspan of 48 inches (122 cm). Ring-billed Gulls are a relatively common and adaptable species, eating a variety of invertebrates and also scavenging on occasions.

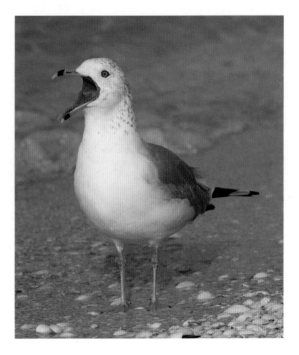

WIDESPREAD The Ring-billed Gull may be the most common North American gull, with its population comprising nearly four million birds.

Forster's Tern

FAMILY Laridae
SPECIES *Sterna forsteri*
LENGTH 14 in (36 cm)
HABITAT Beaches/marshland
CLUTCH SIZE 3–4

DISTRIBUTION Sporadic summer range from Alberta to the northern United States. Occurs along the United States' Pacific and Atlantic coasts and on the Gulf coast.

FORSTER'S TERNS often nest in inland areas in the vicinity of marshes during the summer months, although in some areas, they also breed on the coast. They not only feed on fish, but also invertebrates. The black cap, which is again a feature of these terns, is quite extensive, running back from the bill below the eyes and down the neck. Their wingspan measures 31 inches (79 cm).

COLORATION The bill color of Foster's Tern is yellowish-orange with a fairly prominent dark tip, while the legs are a deeper shade of orange.

Black Tern

FAMILY Laridae
SPECIES *Childonias niger*
LENGTH 9¾ in (25 cm)
HABITAT Lakes/marshland
CLUTCH SIZE 2–3

DISTRIBUTION Breeds from Alberta down across southern Canada to the northern United States, reaching south as far as California, eastward to Colorado. Overwinters in tropical Pacific waters.

THESE TERNS are mainly black in color, with gray wings with a span of 24 inches (61 cm) and a relatively short, forked tail. They also have white undertail coverts. During the winter, the appearance of Black Terns is transformed, so they then appear mainly white, with an area of black plumage on the head and at the shoulders. They are unlikely to be seen in North America at this stage, although occasional individuals have been recorded as overwintering off the Californian coast. Black Terns breed inland, in small colonies using mats of floating vegetation to support their eggs. They feed not by diving, but by hovering and scooping up prey directly from the water's surface. Small fish and invertebrates such as crustaceans feature in their diet.

SURVEYING These birds will catch insects in flight, hawking them in a similar way to swallows.

Atlantic Puffin

FAMILY Alcidae
SPECIES *Fratercula arctica*
LENGTH 12½ in (32 cm)
HABITAT Open sea
CLUTCH SIZE 1

DISTRIBUTION Western Greenland down to the coast of Newfoundland, mainly resident from here to Nova Scotia. Overwinters in the Atlantic and further south, to North Carolina.

THIS IS THE ONLY species of puffin occurring on the Atlantic seaboard of North America. Its brightly colored and large, distinctive bill means that it can be identified easily. These puffins nest in colonies in underground burrows, although they may occasionally nest under rocks. The hen incubates alone, with the male bringing her food. The incubation period lasts for about 30 days, with the young fledging after about seven weeks. The bill is grayish at this stage, and its distinctive coloration develops slowly, over the course of about five years.

MARINE BIRDS Atlantic Puffins live mainly at sea, only coming ashore for breeding purposes each spring, and prefer to nest on islands.

Horned Puffin

FAMILY Alcidae
SPECIES *Fratercula corniculata*
LENGTH 15 in (38 cm)
HABITAT Open sea
CLUTCH SIZE 1

DISTRIBUTION Breeds along the western and southern coasts of Alaska, and through the Aleutians. Overwinters in the Gulf of Alaska westward and southward, on the ocean.

LARGER IN SIZE than its Atlantic counterpart, the Horned Puffin also has a bigger bill. The so-called "horn" is created by the wattle that extends vertically upward from each eye. These disappear at the end of the breeding season and the face becomes significantly darker, being grayish. The bill plates that result in the brightly colored bills of breeding birds of both sexes are also shed at this stage, so the bill assumes a greenish-brown appearance with a dull red tip over the winter. Young birds have a relatively slender grayish-black bill on fledging.

NESTING These puffins nest in colonies, frequently on cliff faces where the hens lay in among the rocks, or sometimes further inland, often under boulders.

COLUMBIFORMES

Pigeons and doves

These birds are generally common, in localities from city centers to rural areas. One of the reasons for their success is their breeding habits. They are opportunistic, nesting whenever conditions are favorable rather than having a set breeding season. They can also rear their young easily. Both members of a pair produce a special protein-rich secretion called crop milk, which they will regurgitate for their offspring. Should a nest fail, however, then a pair will usually start to breed again very quickly afterward. There is no strict division between pigeons and doves—pigeons simply tend to be larger in size.

Rock Dove (or Feral Pigeon)

FAMILY Columbidae
SPECIES *Columba livia*
LENGTH 12½ in (32 cm)
HABITAT Parks/urban areas
CLUTCH SIZE 2

DISTRIBUTION Found throughout the entire continent, as far north as southern Canada, from British Columbia across to Newfoundland. Isolated populations further north.

THIS SPECIES was introduced to the United States from Europe, evolving back from domesticated stock to a free-living existence, which is why these pigeons are now described as feral, hence their alternative name. Nevertheless, they are often seen in close proximity to buildings both in cities and further out in the suburbs. Rock Doves are very effective scavengers, eating virtually anything discarded such as old sandwiches. They often congregate in parks and similar public places, seeking scraps of food from visitors here. They will also descend on bird tables, eating a variety of seeds. They will breed virtually in any month of the year, particularly in southern parts of their range. The cock will pursue his intended mate, engaging in a bowing display. The nest may be built in a tree or shrub, but equally, it may be on an outside ledge or even inside an abandoned building. Both members of the pair take turns incubating their white eggs for a period lasting for two weeks or so.

PLUMAGE In this pair of blue Rock Doves, the larger cock bird (*left*) displays great iridescence.

White-winged Dove

FAMILY Columbidae
SPECIES *Zenaida asiatica*
LENGTH 11½ in (29 cm)
HABITAT Arid areas
CLUTCH SIZE 2

DISTRIBUTION Summer range from southern California and Oklahoma, north to Colorado. Resident further south, and along the Gulf Coast, overwintering here too. Resident in southern Florida.

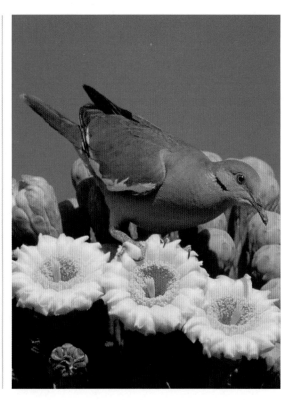

THE RANGE OF THE White-winged Dove varies through the year. They can be recognized by their grayish-brown coloration, and the prominent white areas of plumage running down the outer side of each wing. There is also a bright blue area of bare skin encircling each eye, and the tail is relatively short. Pairs construct a typical flimsy platform of twigs and other vegetation for a nest, often in a tree, but they may alternatively choose a large cactus for this purpose, which gives them added protection against predators. Their eggs will take approximately two weeks to hatch, with the chicks fledging after a similar period.

FEEDING White-winged Doves have a varied diet, feeding not just on seeds of various types, but also on berries and the fruits of cactus.

Mourning Dove

FAMILY Columbidae
SPECIES *Zenaida macroura*
LENGTH 12 in (30 cm)
HABITAT Brushland/suburbs
CLUTCH SIZE 2

DISTRIBUTION Summer range across southern Canada and down into the northern-central United States. Resident in parts of Newfoundland down the east coast, and across much of the United States.

THE MOURNFUL CALLS of this dove account for its common name. Mourning Doves can be sexed by sight, since cock birds are brighter in color than hens, with a pinkish suffusion to the brown feathering on the breast. The lack of blue skin around the eyes, and a longer narrow tail helps to distinguish the Mourning Dove from its White-winged relative in areas where they overlap. Pairs will nest in a bush or tree, and they are likely to rear several broods in succession.

BEHAVIOR Mourning Doves often search for food on the ground and visit bird tables. The spotted patterning on the wings can differ from one individual to another.

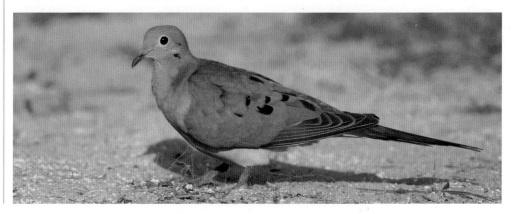

CUCULIFORMES

Cuckoos

One of the best-known characteristics of cuckoos relates to their breeding behavior, as they have a reputation for being brood-parasites, with hens laying their eggs in the nests of other birds. Although many species reproduce in this way, however, some members of this family actually rear their own young. In virtually all cases, although the sexes are similar in appearance, hens can be identified by their slightly larger size. Most birds in this family are distinguished by a fairly slim body shape, long tail, and short legs. They are usually solitary, but their loud calls alert others to their presence.

Black-billed Cuckoo

FAMILY Cuculidae

SPECIES *Coccyzus erythropthalmus*

LENGTH 12 in (30 cm)

HABITAT Woodland near water

CLUTCH SIZE 2–5

DISTRIBUTION Breeds from Nova Scotia to Tennessee. Also westward across to Alberta and Kansas. Overwinters in northern parts of South America.

IDENTIFICATION The bright red area of bare skin encircling the eyes helps to distinguish this species.

THE BLACK-BILLED CUCKOO overlaps in some parts of its range with its Yellow-billed cousin, but it can be distinguished by the color of its upperparts, which are a purer shade of brown. The bill is also black. Young Black-billed Cuckoos have a buff-colored throat and undertail coverts when they first leave the nest, with the white tips to the individual tail feathers being less distinctive. The skin around the eyes is paler in color too. Although these cuckoos are not uncommon in some areas, their population has declined in various parts of their range. It can actually be quite difficult to spot these birds in their woodland habitat, as they are shy by nature. Pairs rear their own young, with the hen laying her eggs on a platform of twigs and leaves in a tree. Incubation lasts for approximately 14 days, and is shared by both parents.

STRIGIFORMES

Owls

Owls have large, rounded faces, with their eyes being directed forward to aid their hunting abilities. Their bills are narrow yet powerful, and they have strong feet equipped with sharp claws that help them to grab their prey. Small rodents are a major item in the diet of many species. Owls are essentially nocturnal hunters, as this is the time when rodents emerge from their daytime hiding places. After eating a meal, an owl regurgitates the skin, bones, and other indigestible remains of its prey. These form a so-called "owl's pellet," confirming the presence of these birds in an area.

Burrowing Owl

FAMILY Strigidae
SPECIES *Speotyto cunicularia*
LENGTH 9½ in (24 cm)
HABITAT Open country
CLUTCH SIZE 5–7

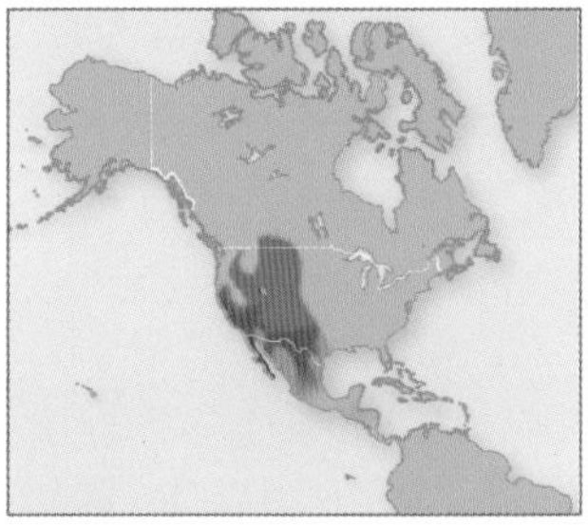

DISTRIBUTION Southern-central Canada through the western United States in the summer. Resident in Florida, and from California along the Mexican border.

THESE OWLS are unusual because they nest underground in suitable burrows, being found in areas where tree cover is scarce. This means that they can range into suburban areas, inhabiting golf courses, for example. They do not tunnel underground themselves, but take over burrows excavated by rodents such as ground squirrels, or may even adopt those dug by gopher tortoises in Florida.

DIET Burrowing Owls catch rodents and invertebrates on the ground. They may be seen on fence posts, scanning the area for prey.

Short-eared Owl

FAMILY Strigidae
SPECIES *Asio flammeus*
LENGTH 15 in (38 cm)
HABITAT Open country
CLUTCH SIZE 5–9

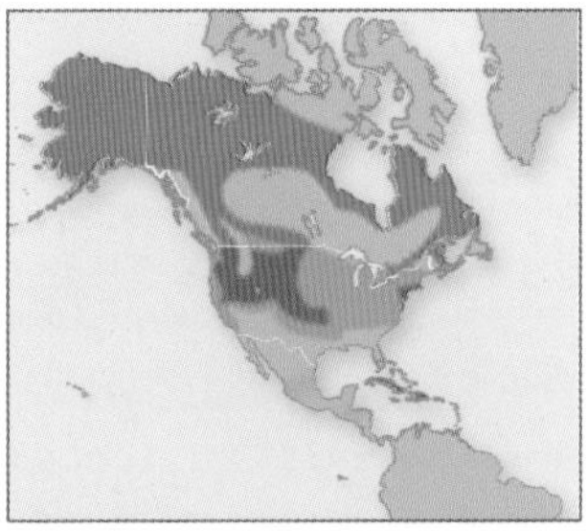

DISTRIBUTION Alaska and most of northern Canada in summer. Resident in northwestern parts of the United States, ranging more widely in winter, but not in the southeast.

THE FACE OF THIS OWL appears rounded, due partly to its very short ear tufts. The Short-eared Owl is a relatively common and also easily seen species, since it is active during the day. In the winter, these owls may form small flocks. They may even hunt collectively, flying back and forth across an area, looking for rodents, which make up the bulk of their diet. Pairs nest on a well-concealed area of ground. The eggs hatch after about three weeks, with the young fledging around six weeks later.

PLUMAGE Mottled brown above, with streaking on the underparts, are identifying characteristics of this species, although the exact patterning differs between individuals.

Barn Owl

FAMILY Strigidae

SPECIES *Tyto alba*

LENGTH 16 in (41 cm)

HABITAT Farmland/cliffs

CLUTCH SIZE 5–11

DISTRIBUTION Resident in western, southern, and eastern areas of the United States, extending further north in the summer, and west to Canada.

ELEGANT AND EASILY IDENTIFIABLE thanks to its distinctive coloration, the Barn Owl may be seen out hunting from dusk onward. The back is tan with grayish markings, with the face and underparts being whitish, with some dark speckling on the underparts. It is possible to sex these owls on the basis of their coloration, since males are lighter in terms of their overall coloration, compared with females. Although the species used to roost on cliffs, it has adapted to the spread of agriculture by adopting barns for this purpose, breeding as well as roosting in this type of environment. The hen incubates the eggs on her own, with hatching taking about 35 days. The young birds should grow rapidly and will leave the nest for the first time once they reach eight weeks of age. Rodents such as rats and mice are their favored prey.

IDENTIFIYING FEATURE The down-curved, sharp but narrow bill of the Barn Owl is clearly apparent here.

Snowy Owl

FAMILY Strigidae

SPECIES *Bubo scandiaca*

LENGTH 23 in (58 cm)

HABITAT Tundra/open country

CLUTCH SIZE 5–9

DISTRIBUTION Ranges extensively across the far north, being resident here on the mainland. Overwinters widely across much of Canada, apart from the east, crossing into the northern United States.

THE SEXES CAN BE distinguished in this species because mature cock birds are almost pure white. In contrast, adult female and young Snowy Owls of both sexes will display quite heavy black barring on their bodies. Living within the Arctic Circle means that during the summer months, when it is permanently light, these owls will often choose to hunt during the day, eating carrion too. In the absence of trees, pairs nest on the ground. The hen incubates the eggs on her own, with hatching taking just over four weeks.

ADAPTATION Feathering continues down to cover the toes, enabling Snowy Owls to walk over snow in the winter and helping to protect them from frostbite.

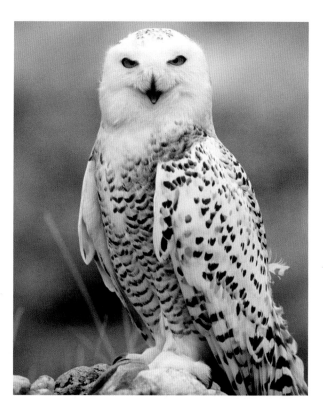

Great Gray Owl

FAMILY Strigidae

SPECIES *Strix nebulosa*

LENGTH 27 in (69 cm)

HABITAT Dense forest

CLUTCH SIZE 2–5

DISTRIBUTION Resident in eastern Alaska and northwestern Canada, south of Hudson Bay, just across the United States' border here. Extends to Wyoming in the west.

AS ITS NAME SUGGESTS, the Great Gray Owl is the largest species of owl occurring in North America. Even the facial disks, which are the flattened areas on each side of the face, are grayish in color, with some darker, concentric markings evident here too. There is a white area on the chin on each side of the face, with a central black area. The narrow bill is a pale shade of greenish-yellow, with the eyes being pale yellow. The plumage on the body is grayish with streaks and barring. Especially in the far north of its range, the Great Gray Owl may be seen hunting during the day, seeking rodents and mice which constitute most of its diet; further south, it is strictly nocturnal, only emerging from its daytime roost under cover of darkness. These owls often take over the nests of birds of prey, although they also nest on cliffs.

DISTINCTIVE SHAPE The flattened, circular face of the Great Gray Owl is clearly apparent in this photograph.

Barred Owl

FAMILY Strigidae

SPECIES *Strix varia*

LENGTH 21 in (53 cm)

HABITAT Dense woodland/ swamp

CLUTCH SIZE 3–4

DISTRIBUTION Ranges from British Columbia eastward to Nova Scotia, down to northern California and southeastern parts of the United States.

BARRING ACROSS the upper chest is very evident in the case of this species, which is brownish-gray in terms of its overall coloration. In contrast, the underparts are streaked. It has a stocky appearance overall, with a short tail. The varied calls of the Barred Owl may reveal its presence in a forest, often being uttered during hours of daylight. Aside from their typical hooting calls, more unusual and distinctive are the cackling notes which these owls often make. Barred Owls feed mainly on mice.

IDENTIFICATION A rounded head, dark eyes, and a relatively pale bill are characteristic features of the Barred Owl. The gray facial disks are highlighted with black borders.

CAPRIMULGIFORMES

Nightjars and nighthawks

As their common name suggests, these birds are shy, and they are secretive in their habits, often nocturnal by nature. They typically emerge under cover of darkness to catch cicadas, moths, and other invertebrates that fly at night. They spend much of the daytime resting on the ground, where their plumage helps to conceal their presence. A remarkable attribute of some species is the way in which they can survive adverse weather conditions, particularly severe cold spells, by becoming torpid. Their metabolism falls but, like hibernating reptiles, they become active again when conditions improve.

Common Nighthawk

FAMILY Caprimulgidae
SPECIES *Chordeiles minor*
LENGTH 9½ in (24 cm)
HABITAT Woodland/suburbs
CLUTCH SIZE 2

DISTRIBUTION Summertime visitor from northern parts of Canada, southward across the entire United States, apart from the southwest. Overwinters in South America, down to Argentina and Uruguay.

BLACKISH-BROWN mottling helps to conceal the presence of this nighthawk, breaking up its profile. Its has a very slender body, accentuated by its long, narrow wings and its forked tail. The hen lacks the white tail band seen in cocks, and has a buff-colored throat, as do young birds. There are some regional variations in coloration too, with those seen in northern parts of North America tending to be relatively gray, while those from the east are browner. Common Nighthawks usually nest on the ground.

BEHAVIOR Common Nighthawks hunt insects in flight, becoming active at dusk and hiding away in vegetation during the daytime.

Common Poorwill

FAMILY Caprimulgidae
SPECIES *Phalaenoptilus nuttallii*
LENGTH 8 in (20 cm)
HABITAT Rocky scrub
CLUTCH SIZE 2

DISTRIBUTION Found over a wide area of western and central parts of the United States in the summer, and may be expanding its range further northeast.

THIS IS THE SMALLEST of the nightjars occurring in North America, and favors open countryside. The majority of the population will retreat southward into Mexico for the winter. Some individuals remain in the United States, however, and they have the ability to become dormant in cold weather, sheltering in among rocks, where they can also remain largely hidden from predators.

CAMOUFLAGE The hunched posture of the Common Poorwill helps it to remain hidden on the ground. It will often hide away under rocks.

APODIFORMES

Hummingbirds

The hummingbirds represent the largest grouping within this Order, comprising some 340 species. They are found only in the Americas, being most numerous in northern South America. Despite their small size, most hummingbirds seen in the United States in summer will fly a considerable distance to their wintering grounds further south. Much of their life is spent in flight. They are also surprisingly aggressive. Their long bils are used to probe flowers for nectar. This sugary solution provides them with a source of energy, while at the same time, they transfer pollen from flower to flower as they feed.

Black-chinned Hummingbird

FAMILY Trochilidae
SPECIES *Archilochus alexandri*
LENGTH 3¾ in (10 cm)
HABITAT Wooded lowland
CLUTCH SIZE 2

DISTRIBUTION Found as far north as southwestern British Columbia in the summer, down through the western parts of the United States into Mexico.

THESE HUMMINGBIRDS begin to arrive in their northern breeding grounds by May, and then start to move south again between August and September. They generally overwinter in Mexico, although individuals may occasionally be seen in southeastern parts of the United States at this stage, too.

DIFFERENCES Only the cock displays the characteristic black plumage on the throat. This area is white in adult hens and the young of both sexes.

Ruby-throated Hummingbird

FAMILY Trochilidae
SPECIES *Archilochus colubris*
LENGTH 3¾ in (10 cm)
HABITAT Gardens
CLUTCH SIZE 2

DISTRIBUTION Occurs widely in eastern North America, and overwinters in Central America from Mexico south to Panama. Rarely seen in Florida in winter.

IN SPITE OF their small size, Ruby-throated Hummingbirds undertake a remarkable journey, migrating back and forth across the Gulf of Mexico every year. In North America, where they spend the summer, they are frequent garden visitors, often attracted by tubular nectar feeders. Like most hummingbirds, however, they are quarrelsome by nature, chasing each other away from the source of food. Males are again also more colorful in appearance than hens.

MATURITY The ruby throat coloration is characteristic of mature males. Young cocks are whitish here until their first winter molt.

Rufous Hummingbird

FAMILY Trochilidae
SPECIES *Selasphorus rufus*
LENGTH 3¾ in (10 cm)
HABITAT Woodland
CLUTCH SIZE 2

DISTRIBUTION Breeds in northwestern North America, overwintering in Mexico, although occasionally recorded in southeastern parts of the United States in winter.

IN THE CASE of this species, and other members of the genus, the typical buzzing sound associated with hummingbirds is created when they are flying rather than hovering. Rufous Hummingbirds are seen in their North American range from the end of February through until September.

COLORATION In keeping with its name, the male of this species is mainly rufous-brown in color.

Calliope Hummingbird

FAMILY Trochilidae
SPECIES *Stellula calliope*
LENGTH 3 in (8 cm)
HABITAT Mountain meadows
CLUTCH SIZE 2

DISTRIBUTION Breeds in inland western North America, and may sometimes be observed through the Great Plains and Texas in the fall; overwinters in Mexico.

THE SMALLEST breeding bird in North America, the Calliope Hummingbird is often to be seen in areas where there are woodland streams close to the upland meadows that provide flowers for these nectar feeders. They can be sexed easily: Although the males do not have a solid area of iridescent plumage forming the gorget, their throat area is clearly streaked with reflective purple.

IDENTIFICATION Hens have bronzy-green spots superimposed on white throat plumage. Young cocks are similar until they molt for the first time.

CORACIIFORMES   Kingfishers

The majority of the ten families forming this Order do not actually occur in North America, although some, such as the todies (Todidae) and motmots (Momotidae), are present elsewhere in the New World. In contrast, hornbills (Bucerotidae) are confined to the Old World. Kingfishers as a group are represented, however, with a small number of species present, but their family is quite widely distributed over the continent. These birds tend to be found close to water. Although small fish are their main quarry, some kingfishers also catch insects, such as dragonflies, that occur in a similar type of environment.

Belted Kingfisher

FAMILY Alcedinidae
SPECIES *Ceryle alcyon*
LENGTH 13 in (33 cm)
HABITAT Near water
CLUTCH SIZE 5–8

DISTRIBUTION Resident in much of Canada, coastal British Columbia, and the western United States; also below South Dakota. It is a winter visitor in the extreme south.

THIS IS THE MOST widely distributed kingfisher in North America, typically inhabiting areas of woodland near water, ranging from streams to lakes. Solitary and territorial by nature, Belted Kingfishers only come together during the breeding season in the spring. Males can be easily distinguished from females by their lack of a rust-red band across the lower belly, so that this part of the body is entirely white. When seeking food, kingfishers have favored vantage points overlooking a stretch of water. Here they will remain, essentially immobile, until a fish or amphibian swims within reach. The kingfisher then dives down into the water, seizing its quarry in its powerful bill.

SOUND ALERT The calls of these kingfishers are loud and quite harsh, usually uttered during flight.

PICIFORMES

Honeyguides, toucans, and woodpeckers

Three families, comprising the toucans (Ramphastidae), honeyguides (Indicatoridae), and woodpeckers (Picidae), make up this Order, but only the latter group occurs in North America. Woodpeckers are remarkably adaptable birds, because although they rely heavily on trees, both for food and nesting, a number are found in arid areas, where they have switched to using giant cacti for these purposes instead. Their claws and tails are sharp, enabling them to anchor on and move easily up a trunk. Furthermore, their bills can be used as drills and chisels, helping them to reach invertebrates lurking around the tree or cactus.

Hairy Woodpecker

FAMILY Picidae
SPECIES *Picoides villosus*
LENGTH 9¼ in (24 cm)
HABITAT Forest
CLUTCH SIZE 4–7

DISTRIBUTION Occurs widely from Alaska to southern New Mexico, and to Newfoundland. Also Florida to eastern-central Texas. Found in Central America.

THE HAIRY WOODPECKER has a white back and its wings are predominantly black but display individual white spotting at the edges. The underparts are also white. On the head there is a broad black stripe running through each eye on males and females, but only the cock birds display a red area on the nape of the neck. This is quite a noisy species, using its bill not just to bore into the bark in search of insect life, but also banging to create a drumming sound. This banging is used by many woodpeckers as a way of marking their territories, although at ground level, it is not always easy to pinpoint the direction of the sound.

HIGH LIFE This adaptable species usually prefers areas of mature woodland, nesting high up in the dead limb of a tree.

Pileated Woodpecker

FAMILY Picidae
SPECIES *Dryocopus pileatus*
LENGTH 16½ in (42 cm)
HABITAT Mature woodland
CLUTCH SIZE 3–5

DISTRIBUTION Found in southern British Columbia to Nova Scotia, and central California, ranging from Illinois to Virginia, Florida, and Texas.

IT IS LIKELY that this is now the largest species of woodpecker occurring in North America, as in spite of a possible recent sighting, the Ivory-billed Woodpecker (*Campephilus principalis*) is believed to be extinct here. The Pileated Woodpecker is predominantly black, with a white stripe on each side of the face, extending down the neck. The plumage under the wings is also white, while the top of the head in both sexes is a brilliant red. This area of plumage is larger in the case of the cock, however, who also displays a red mustache. These woodpeckers favor mature trees, and may be seen in forested areas or more open parkland.

PERMANENT RESIDENTS This species remains resident in an area throughout the year. In the breeding season, they make nests in dead limbs of trees, up to 70 ft (21 m) off the ground.

Yellow-bellied Sapsucker

FAMILY Picidae
SPECIES *Sphyrapicus varius*
LENGTH 8½ in (22 cm)
HABITAT Deciduous forest
CLUTCH SIZE 4–6

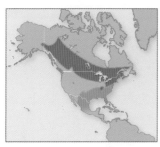

DISTRIBUTION In summer it occurs widely from Alaska to Newfoundland and Nova Scotia. It overwinters in the southeastern United States and into Central America.

THIS SPECIES has yellow colored underparts and a prominent black breast band. Sapsuckers in general have relatively long wings, a characteristic that is emphasized by the long white band running down the edge of the wing. Sapsuckers drill into trees with their bills. This causes the sap to ooze out through the hole, and the sapsucker will drink this regularly as part of its diet.

RED MALE This is the male Yellow-bellied Sapsucker. Hens have white throats and their red plumage is restricted to the crown.

Northern Flicker

FAMILY Picidae
SPECIES *Colaptes auratus*
LENGTH 12½ in (32 cm)
HABITAT Open woodland
CLUTCH SIZE 5–10

DISTRIBUTION Very widely distributed throughout North America: From Alaska and Newfoundland in the north south to the Mexican border.

THE NORTHERN FLICKER is far more widely distributed than the Gilded Flicker. The two species are similar in appearance, to the extent that they used to be considered to be members of the same species. In the Northern Flicker two distinctive color variations are now recognized: Red-shafted and yellow-shafted. Those birds from the north and west of the species' range are yellow-shafted. This is because of the yellow underwing and undertail feathering. Other more evident characteristics in the yellow-shafter variant are the gray plumage on the crown, combined with the tan facial plumage and a red crescent marking on the neck. In the case of the red-shafted variant, the yellow areas are red, the crown is brown, not gray, and there is no red on the nape, but the mustache is red, contrasting with a gray face.

RED-SHAFTED NORTHERN FLICKER This variant occurs in eastern areas, and may interbreed where it meets with yellow-shafted individuals.

PASSERIFORMES

Perching birds

The largest of the avian Orders, the Passeriformes covers a wide range of different genera, found around the world. Some families, such as the tyrant flycatchers (Tyrannidae), which is the largest member of the group, are found exclusively in the New World, whereas others, such as the buntings, grouped in the Family Emberizidae, occur in both the Old and New Worlds. Passeriformes are often small birds, many of which tend to display shades of brown and gray in their plumage, rather than being vividly colored. Many live in flocks.

Olive-sided Flycatcher

FAMILY Tyrannidae
SPECIES *Contopus cooperi*
LENGTH 7½ in (19 cm)
HABITAT Coniferous forest
CLUTCH SIZE 3–4

DISTRIBUTION Breeds on the north and western side of the continent, extending to Newfoundland and down to the Mexican border. Overwinters in Central and South America.

AS THEIR NAME suggests, these flycatchers have olive-gray flanks, with this coloration being separated by a narrow band of white plumage on the chest. They hunt by resting high up in a tree and use the perch here as a vantage point, venturing forth to grab flying insects.

DISTINCTIVE FEATURES Olive-sided Flycatchers are stocky birds, with long wings and a rather short tail.

Western Wood-pewee

FAMILY Tyrannidae
SPECIES *Contopus sordidulus*
LENGTH 6¼ in (16 cm)
HABITAT Woodland
CLUTCH SIZE 3–4

DISTRIBUTION Summer range from southern Alaska through western Canada to California and western Texas, extending into Mexico. Overwinters in northern South America.

THE UNUSUAL NAME of Wood-pewee describes the sound of their calls. Western Wood-pewees have favored perches within their territory, often in exposed positions where they wait, swooping to seize flies and similar insects that come within their reach. When nesting, a pair choose a horizontal branch high up in a tree, about 20 ft (6 m) or more above ground level for their tightly woven nest.

CHICKS IN THE NEST Incubation lasts approximately two weeks, and the young leave the nest by the time they are about 18 days old.

Eastern Phoebe

FAMILY Tyrannidae

SPECIES *Sayornis phoebe*

LENGTH 7 in (18 cm)

HABITAT Woodland

CLUTCH SIZE 3–8

DISTRIBUTION From central Canada southeastward across the United States up to Nova Scotia. Overwinters from North Carolina, through Florida and around the Gulf states to Mexico.

THIS PARTICULAR PHOEBE is often seen in fairly suburban locations, often close to streams and other stretches of water. It collects damp mud when breeding, combining this with moss to build a cup-shaped nest that will be lined with soft down feathers. From a distance, its blackish head and white underparts, sometimes with a pale yellow suffusion in the fall, serve to identify this species. Its bill is black too, and it moves in a jaunty fashion, wagging its tail, and also fanning these feathers as part of a display.

ON WATCH Phoebes are very alert and lively birds by nature, always on the look-out for potential prey. They feed on invertebrates.

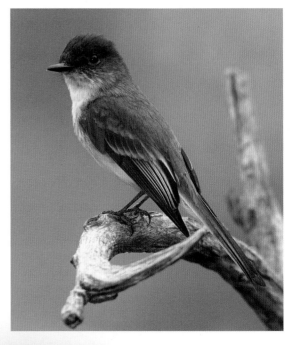

Great Crested Flycatcher

FAMILY Tyrannidae

SPECIES *Myiarchus crinitus*

LENGTH 8 in (20 cm)

HABITAT Open woodland

CLUTCH SIZE 3–7

DISTRIBUTION Eastern North America up to the Great Lakes and to southern Nova Scotia. Overwinters in southern Florida and from southeastern Mexico to northern South America.

AS ITS NAME SUGGESTS, the Great Crested Flycatcher is a relatively large bird. The plumage on its head is olive-gray, with grayish-brown upperparts, while the lower underparts are pale yellow. The tail and flight feathers are reddish-cinnamon, with white barring evident on each wing. Its powerful, pointed bill enables it to grab flying insects easily, although it may eat berries too.

WAITING GAME Great Crested Flycatchers hunt for invertebrates in open woodland, watching and waiting for prey to come within their reach.

Vermilion Flycatcher

FAMILY Tyrannidae
SPECIES *Pyrocephalus rubinus*
LENGTH 6 in (15 cm)
HABITAT Woodland
CLUTCH SIZE 2–3

DISTRIBUTION Summer visitor to the southern United States, generally overwintering to the south in Mexico but may be seen over a wider area in the early fall.

THE STUNNING, VIBRANT coloration of the male Vermilion Flycatcher is instantly recognizable. Hens, in contrast, are much duller, with streaked white markings on the underparts, and a hint of an orange-red wash on the belly itself. Young birds of both sexes resemble the hen, but have a yellower tone to the belly. Immature males start to molt into their adult plumage by the middle of their first winter. The upperparts are a paler shade of brown, compared with the more glossy black appearance of the cock bird. This species is quite common in the United States, although its range is centered mainly on Central America. These birds are usually seen close to water.

SIGHTINGS Vermilion Flycatchers are naturally tame, and quite conspicuous, making them easy to spot as they are frequently observed in the open, on a tree stump or fence post.

Eastern Kingbird

FAMILY Tyrannidae
SPECIES *Tyrannus tyrannus*
LENGTH 8½ in (22 cm)
HABITAT Woodland
CLUTCH SIZE 3–5

DISTRIBUTION Occurs widely through much of North America, up to the Yukon and southern Alaska, with individuals overwintering as far away as Ecuador, Peru, and Brazil.

WHITE UNDERPARTS offset against a dark grayish-black head and wings, with white tips to the tail feathers, help to identify this kingbird. The bill is black, too, and quite stocky. There may be a red area of feathering running across the crown, but this is not generally obvious. These kingbirds are common and conspicuous, often perching in the open. They use this vantage point to look for insects that attract their attention, swooping down to catch any that are within reach. Eastern Kingbirds are highly territorial by nature, and will readily defend an area from incursions by other members of their species, and will also turn on larger birds that may seek to drive them away from a chosen spot. They build relatively bulky nests, made up of vegetable matter, usually high off the ground in a tree. The incubation period lasts from two weeks and the young kingbirds will leave the nest after a similar interval.

FEEDING HABITS It is not just flying insects that will be caught by kingbirds. This particular bird has seized a grasshopper in its long, pointed bill.

Loggerhead Shrike

FAMILY Laniidae
SPECIES *Lanius ludovicianus*
LENGTH 9 in (23 cm)
HABITAT Open country
CLUTCH SIZE 3–8

DISTRIBUTION Summertime visitor in parts of Canada, up to Alberta and Saskatchewan; resident across the United States, down to Florida. May overwinter in Central America.

THE UPPERPARTS of the Loggerhead Shrike are gray, with a prominent black stripe running back from the bill through the eyes on each side of the face; the underparts are white, with a hint of barring. Young birds display more barring on their underparts. The nest itself is built in a tree or bush, with thorny plants being preferred for this purpose.

DIET Feeding largely on insects, Loggerhead Shrikes impale surplus prey on thorns, creating what is known as a larder, where they can return and feed.

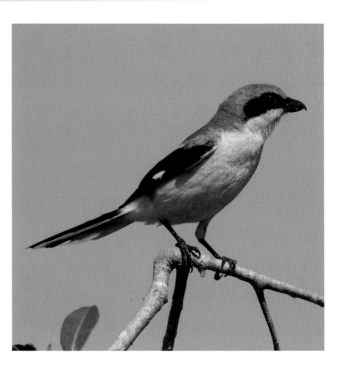

Red-eyed Vireo

FAMILY Vireonidae
SPECIES *Vireo olivaceus*
LENGTH 6 in (15 cm)
HABITAT Woodland
CLUTCH SIZE 3–4

DISTRIBUTION Occurs over a broad area of North America, extending from the west to the east coasts. Ranges from Canada down to the Gulf states.

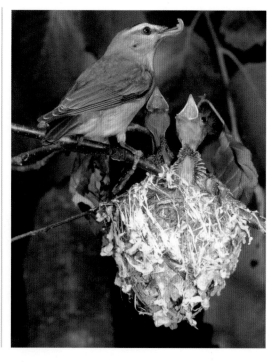

THE DISTINCTIVE red irises of these vireos are striking when seen at close quarters. Unfortunately, like other members of the family, they are not easy to spot, in spite of their relatively large size, as their coloration enables them to merge effectively in among vegetation. Red-eyed Vireos are actually quite common, though, and have extended their range into Oregon in the west and Newfoundland in the east over the course of the past 50 years. In the fall, they fly south again, overwintering in Central America and parts of the Caribbean.

NESTING BEHAVIOR Invertebrates of various types feature prominently in the diet of nestlings. These birds also eat fruit and berries.

Blue Jay

FAMILY Corvidae
SPECIES *Cyanocitta cristata*
LENGTH 11 in (28 cm)
HABITAT Woodland/suburbs
CLUTCH SIZE 3–5

DISTRIBUTION Central and eastern United States to southern Texas; further north in summer in western areas. Year-round in Newfoundland.

THIS IS A COMMON species through its wide range, being conspicuous in part due to its loud calls, although some birds learn the calls of other species as well as their own. They may often be encountered in small groups, in parks and other similar areas of woodland quite close to human habitation. They are often attracted to backyard bird tables in such areas. The Blue Jay's upperparts are bluish, with areas of white in the wings, and they have a crest. The sides of the face are white, with a black collar extending down and around the chest; the rest of the underparts are grayish-white. The stout bill is black, as are the legs and feet. These jays eat a wide variety of foods, taking seeds and nuts, as well as larger invertebrates. When nesting, a pair of birds build a platform-type nest of sticks and other material high up in a tree. The incubation period lasts about 17 days on average.

EGG THIEF Blue Jays are predatory birds, and may raid the nests of songbirds, stealing eggs and young chicks.

American Crow

FAMILY Corvidae
SPECIES *Corvus brachyrhynchos*
LENGTH 17½ in (44 cm)
HABITAT Open country
CLUTCH SIZE 3–6

DISTRIBUTION Found across Canada in summer, but only in southern parts and the United States over the winter; absent from the extreme south.

LARGE IN SIZE and black in color, the American Crow is a common sight over much of North America, especially during the summer months. It has adapted well to changes in the landscape resulting from human activity. These crows used to be found essentially in forested areas, but now they have adapted to thrive in areas of open farmland, and are becoming increasingly common in cities. Social by nature, they tend to nest in colonies, although the number of birds breeding together varies considerably. There may be several hundred in a large colony, which will create a considerable noise, thanks to their loud cawing. American Crows are very watchful, and call to each other at any hint of danger. Their young are reared on a nest of sticks; incubation lasts around 17 days. They fledge once they are about five weeks old.

LARGEST CROW The American Crow is the largest of the crows in North America. Their jet black plumage has a glossy hue, especially on the wings.

Common Raven

FAMILY Corvidae
SPECIES *Corvus corax*
LENGTH 24 in (61 cm)
HABITAT Mountain/desert
CLUTCH SIZE 4–7

DISTRIBUTION Resident all through the far north, right up to Greenland, and down the western side of the United States into Central America.

THE THICKER and heavier bill of ravens is the most obvious point of distinction between crows and ravens. The Common Raven is also much larger overall. It has black plumage, with a glossy hue especially evident over the wings. The feathering in the throat area is relatively long, forming a ruff when it is raised. The Common Raven tends to utter a deep "craak," but it can also display a more varied vocal range. Breeding birds form a life-long pair bond. These corvids occur in a wide range of habitats, and are increasingly common in cities. Although cliffs are still used as nest sites, Common Ravens may also build their nests in trees in parks or high buildings.

NOISE MAKERS These ravens are quite noisy. This one is calling and showing the longer feathering present under the throat.

Horned Lark

FAMILY Alaudidae

SPECIES *Eremophila alpestris*

LENGTH 7¾ in (20 cm)

HABITAT Open country

CLUTCH SIZE 3–5

DISTRIBUTION Through Alaska and much of Canada in the summer, except for central areas. Largely resident further south, but absent from Florida and the adjacent Gulf Coast.

THE PROMINENT BLACK feathering on the head of cock birds looks rather like horns, hence the common name. There are yellow areas evident here too, and a black band across the upper chest. The underparts are whitish, broken by chestnut speckling. Hens are duller in coloration than their mates. The Horned Lark is the only species of lark occurring in North America, being found over almost the entire continent. They forage for food on the ground, seeking seeds as well as invertebrates, and may sometimes be seen close to buildings, including airport terminals. Pairs also nest in these surroundings, with the eggs being laid in a scrape, lined with vegetation. The hen sits alone, and the young hatch in 12 days, and fledge after a similar period. Groups of these larks often congregate during the fall, forming large flocks over the winter in some areas.

GROUND BIRD The Horned Lark spends much of its time on the ground, sometimes running in pursuit of invertebrate prey.

Tree Swallow

FAMILY Hirundinidae

SPECIES *Tachycineta bicolor*

LENGTH 5¾ in (14 cm)

HABITAT Woodland near water

CLUTCH SIZE 4–6

DISTRIBUTION Breeds across northern and central North America; tends to be absent in the south. Overwinters by the coast. Resident in California.

THE METALLIC BLUISH-BLACK coloration of the Tree Swallow is very evident on the head and upperparts, contrasting with the pure white on the throat and underparts. The wings are both broad and very long, reaching beyond the tip of the tail. These birds nest widely across much of North America, breeding in natural tree hollows, adopting the abandoned nests of a woodpecker, or even occupying nestboxes. Each fall, large flocks of these swallows congregate before undertaking the journey to their southern wintering grounds.

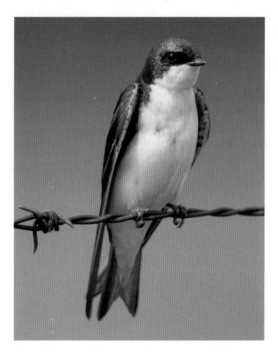

SELECTION OF PERCHES Tree Swallows may be seen perching on wire fences as here, or on telephone lines. They hunt invertebrates, but will eat berries occasionally.

Purple Martin

FAMILY Hirundinidae
SPECIES *Progne subis*
LENGTH 7½ in (19 cm)
HABITAT Woodland/suburbs
CLUTCH SIZE 3–6

DISTRIBUTION Summer visitor from Canada to Florida. Sporadic elsewhere, seen especially in southwestern states and on the west coast. Overwinters in northern South America.

RELATIVELY DULL IN COLOR, in spite of its name, the Purple Martin is the largest species of swallow occurring in North America. Cock birds display glossy bluish-black upperparts, with the iridescence being greatest over the head. Hens and young birds of both sexes are dusky black above and a lighter, grayish shade below. They hunt invertebrates in flight, flying fast and then gliding in short bursts. Purple Martins may be seen quite commonly in urban areas, often nesting under the eaves of buildings, although hollow trees are more traditional. The hen incubates the eggs alone, with hatching occurring after about 16 days. The young martins fledge at about a month old.

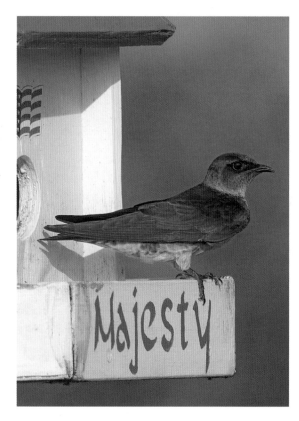

URBAN HOMES Manmade structures, such as this purpose-built martin house, provide these birds with suburban nesting opportunities.

Northern Rough-winged Swallow

FAMILY Hirundinidae
SPECIES *Stelgidopteryx serripennis*
LENGTH 5 in (13 cm)
HABITAT Cliffs/riverbanks
CLUTCH SIZE 4–8

DISTRIBUTION All over North America, from British Columbia south, in summer. Overwinters in southern Florida. Resident on the southern Texas border.

THESE SWALLOWS are so-called because of the small rough hooks present on the leading outer edge of each of the longest flight feathers, the function of which is unclear. The sexes are similar in appearance and dull in coloration: The upperparts are brown, while the underparts are paler, with a grayish-brown suffusion across the chest. These swallows migrate in small groups, rather than as large flocks.

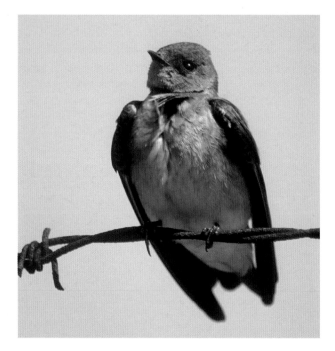

SHORT TAILS This swallow species has a very short, square tail. The sexes are similar in appearance but young birds have cinnamon wing bars.

Barn Swallow

FAMILY Hirundinidae
SPECIES *Hirundo rustica*
LENGTH 6¾ in (17 cm)
HABITAT Buildings
CLUTCH SIZE 3–6

DISTRIBUTION Ranges from southern Alaska southeastward and south, over virtually the whole continent. Absent in parts of the extreme southwest and southern Florida.

OUT OF ALL the swallows, it is this species that has become most closely identified with human settlements in North America. The Barn Swallow breeds in colonies, attaching its nest of mud and dry grass to a vertical surface such as the wall of a building or a bridge. In the past, these birds used to nest in hollow trees, but buildings are now used far more frequently. It is impossible to distinguish the sexes by sight, but the appearance of the Barn Swallow is such that it cannot be confused with any other swallow species. The wings are long, as is the deeply forked tail, which may sometimes appear just as a single streamer if the tail feathers are kept closed.

ON THE WING Barn Swallows are a glossy bluish-black shade and have a small chestnut area above the bill.

Bank Swallow

FAMILY Hirundinidae
SPECIES *Riparia riparia*
LENGTH 4¾ in (12 cm)
HABITAT Riverbanks
CLUTCH SIZE 4–6

DISTRIBUTION From Alaska to Newfoundland and south across much of the northern United States; generally absent from the south, with the exception of the southern Texas border.

THE COLORATION of the Bank Swallow is quite plain, with the upperparts being brown, and the lowerparts white, apart from a dark brown band across the chest. This is also the smallest North American swallow, and is usually associated with river banks, where it nests in large colonies. Instead of building a nest, these swallows tunnel into the soft earth, to construct a burrow that enlarges into a nesting chamber at its end. This chamber is lined with feathers and vegetation. Swallow pairs return to the same nesting areas every year.

RIVERSIDE HOME The chicks spend three weeks in the nest. When they emerge, they can be distinguished at first by buff wing bars.

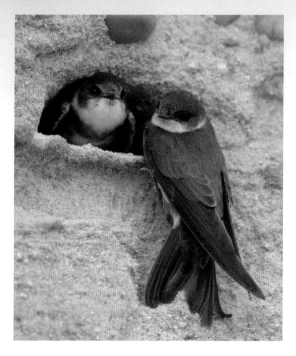

Black-capped Chickadee

FAMILY Paridae
SPECIES *Parus atricapillus*
LENGTH 5¼ in (13 cm)
HABITAT Woodland
CLUTCH SIZE 4–8

DISTRIBUTION Resident in a southeasterly direction across the continent to Newfoundland, south to northern California in the west, and as far south as northern New Mexico.

THIS IS NOT THE ONLY chickadee with a black cap on its head; where their distribution overlaps, it is difficult to distinguish this species and the Carolina Chickadee by appearance only. It is possible on the basis of size, however, since the Black-capped Chickadee is larger. Another point of distinction, particularly after the molt, is the white edging that this species has on its secondary wing feathers. Active by nature, Black-capped Chickadees often visit backyard feeders, with sunflower seed kernels being a particular favorite. They breed in tree holes, and sometimes adopt nestboxes. An assortment of plant matter and feathers is used to line the interior of the nest.

BLACK AND WHITE The black throat patch and white face of the Black-capped Chickadee are clearly evident from this angle. The underparts of the body are a creamy shade.

Tufted Titmouse

FAMILY Paridae
SPECIES *Parus bicolor*
LENGTH 6½ in (17 cm)
HABITAT Woodland
CLUTCH SIZE 5–8

DISTRIBUTION Found year-round in southeastern parts, from the area around the Great Lakes westward to Oklahoma and through eastern Texas. Absent from southern Florida.

THIS SPECIES can vary in the color of its tufted crest and its forehead. Some individuals have a gray crest with a black area above the bill, while others have a blackish crest and much paler forehead coloration. The underparts are always whitish, with a slight buffy hue apparent on the flanks. The Tufted Titmouse is social by nature, sometimes seen foraging in mixed groups alongside other similar species, looking for invertebrates in among the branches of trees and shrubs.

BIRDSONG The cock bird of this species is a very talented songster, with a surprisingly varied range of different song patterns.

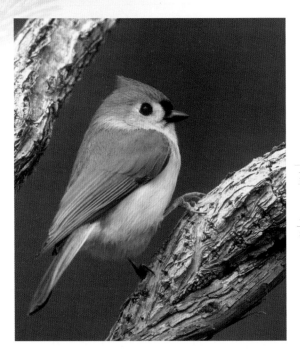

Red-breasted Nuthatch

FAMILY Sittidae
SPECIES *Sitta canadensis*
LENGTH 4½ in (11 cm)
HABITAT Woodland
CLUTCH SIZE 5–8

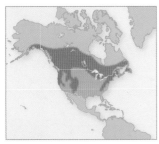

DISTRIBUTION Occurs in southern Canada, breeding further north in the summer. It can be seen virtually anywhere in the United States in winter but is absent from Florida.

NUTHATCHES ARE FOUND in woodland areas, scurrying up and down the trunk with remarkable agility. The Red-breasted Nuthatch tends to favor coniferous forest. It is possible to distinguish the sexes by their appearance. Cock birds have a black cap, with white stripes beneath, running above the eye. There is a black stripe across the eyes; the underparts are rusty-red, and the back and wings are bluish-gray. Hens have a slate-gray rather than a black cap; this coloration is also seen in young birds of both sexes. Pairs of this species may breed in tree hollows up to 100 ft (30 m) off the ground.

NOT ONLY NUTS These nuthatches feed on conifer seeds, which form a major part of their diet over the winter, and invertebrates.

White-breasted Nuthatch

FAMILY Sittidae
SPECIES *Sitta carolinensis*
LENGTH 5¾ in (14 cm)
HABITAT Woodland
CLUTCH SIZE 5–9

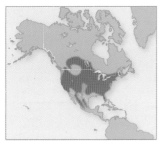

DISTRIBUTION Resident in southern Canada, and western parts of the United States. Also occurs widely in the eastern United States, but absent from Florida and the Gulf Coast.

SHARP PROBE The narrow beak of the White-breasted Nuthatch allows it to probe small holes in the bark and seize its prey without difficulty.

THIS PARTICULAR nuthatch can be identified quite easily, as it is the only species with a white face. This coloration also extends down on to the underparts. The crown and nape are black, with the back and wings being bluish-gray. It has a wide distribution, and is found in both broadleaf and coniferous woodland, although it generally inhabits mature trees. In common with other nuthatches, the agile White-breasted Nuthatch hunts invertebrates partly by pausing at regular intervals, to watch for any signs of movement in its vicinity.

Brown Creeper

FAMILY Certhidae

SPECIES *Certhia americana*

LENGTH 5¼ in (13 cm)

HABITAT Woodland

CLUTCH SIZE 4–8

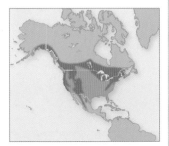

DISTRIBUTION From southern Alaska via Arizona and New Mexico into Mexico. Breeds across southern Canada; resident east of the Great Lakes. Widespread over winter.

THE MOTTLED PLUMAGE on the back and wings of the Brown Creeper enables it to blend very effectively against the bark of most trees. The tail feathers are quite rigid at their tips, tapering to a point, and they help to support these birds when they are climbing up tree trunks. Just as with woodpeckers, however, this characteristic prevents them from moving head-first downward.

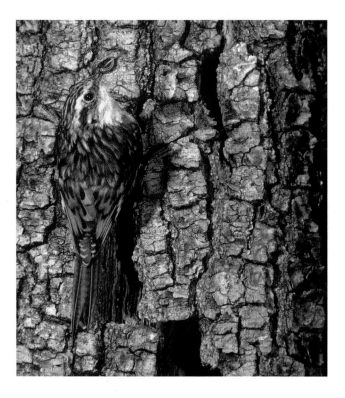

NARROW BILL The Brown Creeper has a narrow, down-curving bill, allowing it to probe into cracks in the bark and extract invertebrates easily.

Rock Wren

FAMILY Troglodytidae

SPECIES *Salpinctes obsoletus*

LENGTH 6 in (15 cm)

HABITAT Arid country

CLUTCH SIZE 4–7

DISTRIBUTION Resident from California southeast to Texas. Breeds to the north and east of this, reaching southwestern Canada and south through the Dakotas to Oklahoma.

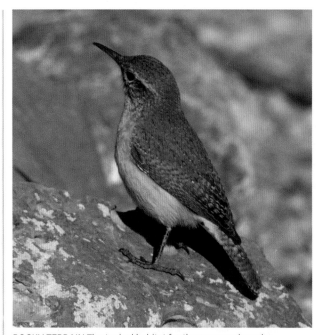

ROCKY TERRAIN The typical habitat for these wrens is rocky scrubland or desert areas where there are boulders. Their coloration helps them to blend in.

ROCK WRENS are quite conspicuous birds, they are often seen out in the open and usually bobbing up and down along the ground. The bill is long, narrow, and curves down slightly toward the tip, allowing these wrens to reach invertebrates concealed under rocks or in small crevices. A breeding pair will often choose to nest in a rocky outcrop too, constructing their nest using dry vegetation and other items such as wool or hair, and then lining the structure with soft feathers. The hen sits alone, while the cock bird may build a path of small stones leading to the nest, revealing its location for reasons that are unclear.

Marsh Wren

FAMILY Troglodytidae
SPECIES *Cistothorus palustris*
LENGTH 5 in (13 cm)
HABITAT Marshland
CLUTCH SIZE 5–9

DISTRIBUTION Resident in the west; absent from central and eastern United States; spends winter in the south. Breeds from western Canada east via the Great Lakes to Nova Scotia.

ALTHOUGH SMALL and also quite inconspicuous birds in terms of their coloration, Marsh Wrens have a powerful song that belies their size, as in the case of many wrens. They may often be heard singing from the depths of a reed bed, but pinpointing their location can be difficult. Marsh Wrens are predominantly brown in color. They have a prominent brown cap with a white stripe running back above the eye; the underparts are pale in color. The back and wings are blackish, with white striping. The sexes are identical in appearance. Marsh Wrens hunt midges and other invertebrates living in their damp habitat, sometimes catching their prey on the surface of the water. Pairs build a ball-shaped nest of reeds, anchored just above the waterline.

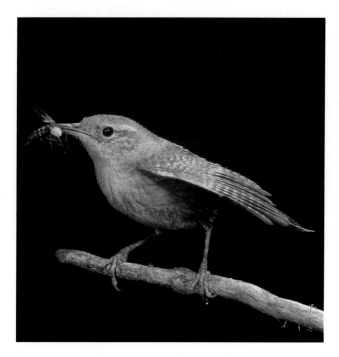

COCKED TAIL Many wren species typically perch with their tail feathers vertical, as shown here by this Marsh Wren.

House Wren

FAMILY Troglodytidae
SPECIES *Troglodytes aedon*
LENGTH 4¾ in (12 cm)
HABITAT Buildings/parks
CLUTCH SIZE 3–6

DISTRIBUTION Breeds across southern Canada and most of the United States. Resident in California and from Alabama east to North Carolina. Spends winter in the southern states.

THIS IS ONE of the most conspicuous wrens, as it often occurs in backyards and city areas. It has a rich, bubbling song that often emanates from undergrowth without the bird being visible. Its upperparts are grayish-brown, with this coloration extending down on both sides of the head to the vicinity of the throat; just the hint of an eyebrow stripe is evident.

TASTY MEAL House Wrens forage for invertebrates in gardens and parks. They breed in nestboxes, tree hollows, or holes in walls.

American Dipper

FAMILY Cinclidae

SPECIES *Cinclus mexicanus*

LENGTH 7½ in (19 cm)

HABITAT Mountain streams

CLUTCH SIZE 3–6

DISTRIBUTION Occurs down the western side of North America extending from Alaska south to California. Found as far south as Panama in Central America in suitable habitat.

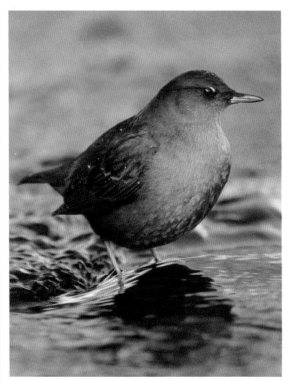

WADING IN WATER These birds walk in a jaunty manner, particularly when in water. Water runs off their plumage readily.

THE AMERICAN DIPPER is only ever likely to be encountered in the vicinity of fast-flowing streams in mountain areas. It has a somewhat stocky appearance, and is slate-gray in color overall, with yellow legs and a relatively dark bill. Its name comes partly from the way it moves in and out of the water, often traveling on foot, hopping from one partially submerged rock to another along the stream, even in proximity to a waterfall. American Dippers are solitary birds by nature, with pairs only coming together to nest in the spring. The nest is well-concealed, sometimes being built under a manmade structure, such as a bridge. The hen sits alone on the eggs for just over two weeks, with the young dippers fledging when they are just over three weeks old.

Ruby-crowned Kinglet

FAMILY Regulidae

SPECIES *Regulus calendula*

LENGTH 4¼ in (11 cm)

HABITAT Woodland

CLUTCH SIZE 5–11

DISTRIBUTION This is a summer visitor from Alaska via Hudson Bay to the east coast. It overwinters in central, western, and southern areas, down into Central America.

ONLY THE COCK BIRD displays the bright red area on the crown that typifies this kinglet, and this area will only be evident if these feathers are raised. Ruby-crowned Kinglets are not easy birds to observe, partly because of their rather subdued coloration, but also because they live high up in the trees, largely out of sight from the ground.

HARD WINTERS Kinglets may struggle to find insects, which form the basis of their diet, in winter. They are more likely to be seen at this time.

American Robin

FAMILY Turdidae
SPECIES *Turdus migratorius*
LENGTH 10 in (25 cm)
HABITAT Woodland
CLUTCH SIZE 3–4

DISTRIBUTION Breeding range extends through Canada, and it is resident through the United States. Winters in Florida and in southern California and Texas.

THE BEAUTIFUL COLORATION of the American Robin helps to make these members of the thrush family easy to identify. The reddish-orange of the underparts contrasts with the grayish-brown upperparts. There is white plumage around the eyes, and streaking on the throat, with the plumage on the head being of a blackish shade. As is often the case, the hens are less brightly colored. The American Robin is a very adaptable species, and bold by nature, being observed in a range of different habitats. These birds are common backyard visitors, being attracted by bird-table offerings during the winter months, and may also hunt for worms on the lawn. When breeding, they often choose a forked branch on which they construct a cup-shaped nest, but may sometimes use an accessible shelf in an outbuilding instead.

BERRY FEAST In the fall, berries feature prominently in the diet of American Robins. The seach for this food can draw birds into gardens at this time of year.

Hermit Thrush

FAMILY Turdidae
SPECIES *Catharus guttatus*
LENGTH 6¾ in (17 cm)
HABITAT Woodland
CLUTCH SIZE 3–5

DISTRIBUTION Breeds from Alaska east to Newfoundland, and south to Texas. Resident on west and east coasts. Spends winter across the south and southeast to Central America.

VARIED DIET Hermit Thrushes eat berries, as well as hunting for earthworms, spiders, and similar creatures on or near the forest floor.

THE HERMIT THRUSH is a common species, but it is more likely to be noticed by the sound of its song emanating from undergrowth rather than by being seen. Its upperparts are olive-brown, with blackish-brown spotting across its pale chest, with these markings fading over the abdomen. The flanks have a grayish suffusion, helping to distinguish this species from other similarly marked thrushes.

Swainson's Thrush

FAMILY Turdidae
SPECIES *Catharus ustulatus*
LENGTH 7 in (18 cm)
HABITAT Woodland
CLUTCH SIZE 3–5

DISTRIBUTION Breeds from Alaska across Canada, down to California in the west, and the vicinity of the Great Lakes in the east. Overwinters in northern South America.

THESE THRUSHES ARE relatively common through their range in North America during the summer breeding season, frequenting damp woodland areas. When they head south for winter, they generally migrate under cover of darkness rather than during the day. This species is similar in appearance to other members of the genus, but it is olive-brown overall, with those individuals from western areas being of a more reddish-brown shade. They feed on the ground, sometimes turning over vegetation with their bills in search of invertebrates.

SONGBIRD Like many thrushes, Swainson's Thrush has an attractive song. Cock birds sing most frequently at the start of the nesting period.

Western Bluebird

FAMILY Turdidae

SPECIES *Sialia mexicana*

LENGTH 7 in (18 cm)

HABITAT Woodland/open
country

CLUTCH SIZE 4–6

DISTRIBUTION Breeds in
southern British Columbia into
California, and in Colorado.
Overwinters over a broad area:
Arizona, New Mexico, and Texas.

A DEEP BLUE COLOR is
characteristic of the Western
Bluebird male, which has
chestnut areas on the
underparts and sides of the
body and a bluish-gray belly.
Hens are not so brightly
colored, being brownish-
gray above, with a grayish
throat, and a chestnut
suffusion on the chest.
Especially after the breeding
season, Western Bluebirds
can be seen in large flocks.

MUSICAL SONG Like related species,
these bluebirds have an attractive
song, heard most often at the start
of the breeding season. This is a male.

Eastern Bluebird

FAMILY Turdidae

SPECIES *Sialia sialis*

LENGTH 7 in (18 cm)

HABITAT Woodland/open
country

CLUTCH SIZE 2–7

DISTRIBUTION Breeds in the
north, to southeastern Canada.
Resident from Maine to north
Texas. Overwinters further to
the southeast, and in southern
Arizona. Not in southern Florida.

THESE BLUEBIRDS ARE SIMILAR in appearance to related
species; rusty upperparts and a white belly are identifying
features of the cock bird. Pairs will often adopt nestboxes,
although they traditionally breed in tree holes, creating a
cup-shaped nest made largely with grass.

VARIED MENU Eastern
bluebirds hunt insects and
also visit bird tables. Young
birds are brownish in color.

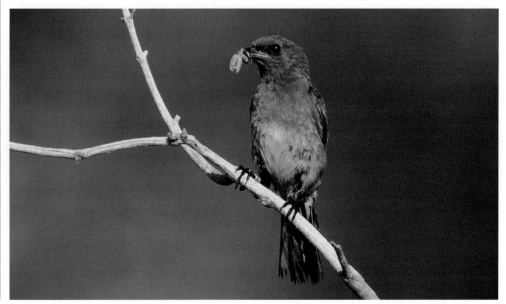

Gray Catbird

FAMILY Mimidae

SPECIES *Dumetella carolinensis*

LENGTH 8½ in (22 cm)

HABITAT Woodland/shrubland

CLUTCH SIZE 3–5

DISTRIBUTION Eastern United States in the summer, north to Yukon and Nova Scotia. Resident down the east coast and across the southern states, wintering on the Gulf Coast.

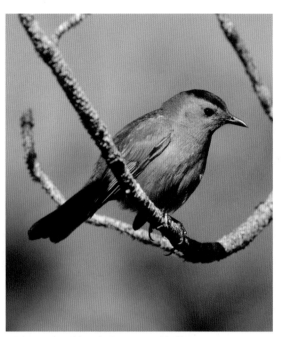

GOOD MIMIC Although the Gray Catbird is a common summer visitor over a wide area of North America, its unusual calls may mean that its presence is sometimes overlooked.

GRAY COLORING predominates in this species and overall its appearance is very subdued, although it has a black area on the head, contrasting with the surrounding gray plumage, and chestnut-red undertail coverts. What sets it apart, however, is the sound of its calls. These are like the miaowing of a cat, which can create considerable confusion in the suburban areas where it often occurs. In addition, the aptly named Gray Catbird is also able to mimic the sounds of other birds in its immediate environment, potentially resulting in further confusion. During the breeding season, pairs nest in a suitable thicket, building a cup-shaped nest.

Northern Mockingbird

FAMILY Mimidae

SPECIES *Mimus polyglottos*

LENGTH 10 in (25 cm)

HABITAT Woodland/shrubland

CLUTCH SIZE 3–5

DISTRIBUTION Resident across many of the southern states, from Nova Scotia to New Mexico and west to California. Also breeds further north in midwestern states.

THE NATURAL SOUND of the Northern Mockingbird's song is attractive and loud, although these birds also prove to be talented mimics, picking up the calls of other species with ease. Their plumage is quite dull in color, with gray upperparts and white underparts. The white areas in the wings are evident when they are in flight. They can also be seen when these birds are foraging, as they often flash their wings during their search for invertebrates. They have adapted well to the suburbs, where there are trees and shrubs to serve as nest sites, and feeding opportunities on the lawn.

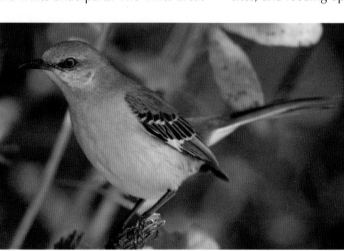

COCKED TAIL As with wrens, this mocking bird often raises its long tail feathers when on the move, revealing the white feathers underneath.

Brown Thrasher

FAMILY Mimidae

SPECIES *Toxostoma rufum*

LENGTH 11½ in (29 cm)

HABITAT Thicket/woodland

CLUTCH SIZE 2–4

DISTRIBUTION Eastern half of the United States, northwest to Alberta in Canada during the summer. Resident along the eastern coast and through the southeastern United States.

UNLIKE MANY THRASHERS, this species has a comparatively short and stocky bill. The upperparts are reddish-brown with two white bars with darker edging above running across each wing. There are pale areas around the eyes as well, with thin streaking on the sides of the face. Elongated dark blotches are evident on the white underparts. Cock birds can be distinguished by their song at the start of the breeding season, often singing from a conspicuous branch. The nest itself is built on or near the ground.

BRAVE FORAGER This species can be bold, venturing into backyards where they forage for berries.

Sage Thrasher

FAMILY Mimidae

SPECIES *Oreoscoptes montanus*

LENGTH 8½ in (22 cm)

HABITAT Sagebrush/juniper

CLUTCH SIZE 4–5

DISTRIBUTION Southwestern Canada to northern Arizona and New Mexico. Overwinters in California and further south to Texas and Mexico.

RELATIVELY SMALL IN SIZE, with a short black bill, the Sage Thrasher spends its summers in the sagebrush flats where it breeds. It usually lives close to the ground, flying or running back to cover when startled or disturbed. Its upperparts are grayish-brown, with the underparts being grayish-white, broken by brownish speckling. During the winter, it inhabits juniper woodland.

SAGE AND JUNIPER This thrasher is linked with specific habitats through the year, although it may also be observed in backyards.

American Pipit

FAMILY Motacillidae

SPECIES *Anthus rubescens*

LENGTH 6½ in (17 cm)

HABITAT Tundra/open country

CLUTCH SIZE 3–7

DISTRIBUTION Breeds in Alaska and northern Canada, as well as southwestern parts of the United States to central Arizona. Overwinters in the southern states, into Mexico.

THE AMERICAN PIPIT spends much of its time on the ground, walking rather than hopping. Its long tail twitches up and down as it moves in this way. Their appearance varies through the year. They have grayish-brown upperparts when they are on their breeding grounds in the far north, with only faint streaking on the underparts; they become browner in color and display more conspicuous markings on their underparts in winter, when they are most likely to be encountered in flocks in open country, and sometimes venture into coastal areas. Pairs nest on the ground, lining a scrape with soft material as insulation for their brown-speckled, whitish eggs. The hen sits alone, with the young hatching after two weeks and fledging after a similar period.

DIET OF BUGS The short, slender bill of the American Pipit is used to catch the small invertebrates that form its diet.

European Starling

FAMILY Sturnidae

SPECIES *Sturnus vulgaris*

LENGTH 8½ in (22 cm)

HABITAT Urban areas/ farmland

CLUTCH SIZE 5–6

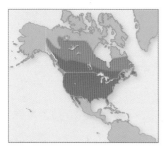

DISTRIBUTION Throughout the United States and much of Canada, being a summer visitor to northern parts. One of the most widely distributed birds.

THIS HIGHLY ADAPTABLE species was first brought to the United States in the 1890s, being liberated in New York. Since then, European Starlings have spread right across the continent and up into the far north. Their appearance is unmistakable, as they have blackish plumage with greenish-purple iridescence and brownish speckling, becoming duller over the winter. Young birds are grayish-brown overall.

NOT FUSSY Berries, insects, and bird-table fare are all readily consumed by European Starlings, which may sometimes form large flocks.

Cedar Waxwing

FAMILY Bombycillidae

SPECIES *Bombycilla cedrorum*

LENGTH 7¼ in (18 cm)

HABITAT Woodland

CLUTCH SIZE 3–6

DISTRIBUTION Seen in summer across southern Canada, resident across the northern half of the United States, also overwintering further south, down into Central America as far as Panama.

WAXWINGS ARE so-called because of the reddish areas at the back of the wings, which resemble sealing wax in appearance. They feed mainly on berries, and breed relatively late in the year for this reason. Although traditionally associated with woodlands, Cedar Waxwings are now being seen increasingly in backyards, being attracted here to feed on the berries of exotic plants. They can be sexed on the basis of the black plumage present under the bill—this is more extensive in cock birds. Young Cedar Waxwings can be recognized by their streaked underparts and duller appearance overall. Social by nature, these waxwings may be seen in large flocks over the fall and winter.

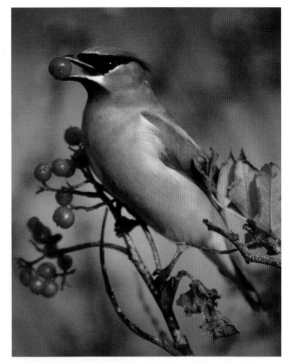

FEEDING Waxwings will pluck individual berries using their pointed bill, and swallow each one in turn. They also catch invertebrates on occasions, and may eat flowers.

Bohemian Waxwing

FAMILY Bombycillidae

SPECIES *Bombycilla garrulus*

LENGTH 8¼ in (21 cm)

HABITAT Woodland

CLUTCH SIZE 4–6

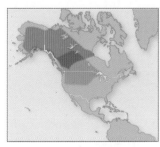

DISTRIBUTION Summer visitor, from Alaska southeast to Hudson Bay. Resident further south in Canada, and seen in western areas of the United States over the winter.

THE CREST FEATHERS of the Bohemian Waxwing may trail back low over the head, only being raised when the individual is alert. This species is larger than the Cedar Waxwing, and has gray rather than yellowish underparts. Pairs may rear their chicks as high as 50 ft (15 m) up in a conifer, using a horizontal branch to help in supporting the nest. This is made from twigs, with the interior being lined with softer material such as moss. The incubation and fledging periods will both last approximately two weeks.

DIET The Bohemian Waxwing no longer relies just on native North American plants, eating the berries of introduced backyard plants, too.

Cerulean Warbler

FAMILY Parulidae

SPECIES *Dendroica cerulea*

LENGTH 4¾ in (12 cm)

HABITAT Woodland near water

CLUTCH SIZE 4–5

DISTRIBUTION Summer visitor to the area of the Great Lakes southward, reaching Alabama, and west to eastern Oklahoma. Winters across northwestern South America to Bolivia.

THESE WOOD-WARBLERS live high up in tall trees where they hunt invertebrates, sometimes catching them in the air. Their breeding habits are hard to observe, as a pair may construct their nest at a height of up to 100 ft (30 m) above the ground. The hen incubates alone, with young Cerulean Warblers of both sexes resembling hens on fledging.

COLOR DIFFERENCES The cock Cerulean Warbler has vivid sky-blue plumage on the head and upperparts, in contrast to the greenish-blue coloration of hens.

Yellow-rumped Warbler

FAMILY Parulidae

SPECIES *Dendroica coronata*

LENGTH 5½ in (14 cm)

HABITAT Woodland/parks

CLUTCH SIZE 4–5

DISTRIBUTION Widely distributed from Alaska across Canada to Newfoundland. Resident in areas of the west coast and southwest. Overwinters in the southeast and southern parts.

AS WITH A NUMBER of the warblers, there has been much debate about the correct taxonomy for this species. The Yellow-rumped Warbler is the result of interbreeding between two separate species, occurring widely across the continent and known as the Myrtle Warbler and Audubon's Warbler.

PLUMAGE Both cock and hen birds in breeding condition display the characteristic yellow plumage on the rump.

Yellow-throated Warbler

FAMILY Parulidae

SPECIES *Dendroica dominica*

LENGTH 5½ in (14 cm)

HABITAT Woodland

CLUTCH SIZE 4–5

DISTRIBUTION Eastern United States, south of the Great Lakes in summer. Resident on the Gulf Coast and Florida, overwintering in southern Florida, the Caribbean, and Central America.

THESE WARBLERS are found primarily in sycamore woods and pine-oak forests. They breed high up in the treetops, and have an unusual way of foraging for food here. Yellow-throated Warblers will probe the bark for invertebrates using their long bill, and move slowly along the branches, to catch their prey unawares. Various localized races are recognized through their range, with birds from western areas tending to have a pure white stripe above the eyes.

COLORATION
The bright yellow plumage of this species extends down on to the underparts, while the back is grayish.

Yellow Warbler

FAMILY Parulidae

SPECIES *Dendroica petechia*

LENGTH 5 in (13 cm)

HABITAT Willow/wet woodland

CLUTCH SIZE 4–5

DISTRIBUTION Through much of North America including the south and southeastern United States. Overwinters in the south, down to Brazil.

YELLOW PLUMAGE predominates in this species, with the wings and tail being more of an olive shade. Cock birds are more brightly colored than hens, with chestnut stripes on the breast and flanks. Yellow Warblers breed across much of North America in the summer months and are likely to be seen in areas of open woodland, usually close to water. Here they move through the foliage in search of invertebrates. When breeding, they build a deep cup-shaped nest for their eggs, which usually hatch after 10 days or so.

DISTANT TRAVELS These birds may fly long distances every year from their southern winter homes to their breeding grounds.

Black-and-white Warbler

FAMILY Parulidae
SPECIES *Mniotilta varia*
LENGTH 5½ in (14 cm)
HABITAT Woodland
CLUTCH SIZE 4–5

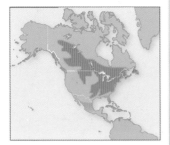

DISTRIBUTION Widespread across central North America and southeast to Texas. Seen in coastal areas of the southeast in winter, through Central America and the Caribbean.

IN THE BREEDING season, the male of this species is characterized by his pied plumage. The throat and cheeks are black; the chin becomes white during the winter. Hens have buffy-colored plumage on their flanks, with gray streaking being apparent here as well. These warblers are unusual in that they will search for invertebrates on tree trunks, not just on branches.

INSECT-LOVER This species tends to be less active than other warblers, using its long bill to probe in bark for invertebrates of various types.

Ovenbird

FAMILY Parulidae
SPECIES *Seiurus aurocapillus*
LENGTH 6 in (15 cm)
HABITAT Forest
CLUTCH SIZE 4–6

DISTRIBUTION Occurs in the southeast across central North America into northern Alabama and Georgia. Overwinters in southern Florida and southern Texas southward.

THE UNUSUAL NAME of the Ovenbird results from the dome-shaped nest that it builds in a concealed area on the forest floor. These birds are largely terrestrial in their habits, walking with their tail feathers held in a semi-vertical posture. They live mainly on invertebrates.

PLUMAGE The Ovenbird has a black stripe on each side of the head, bordering the rusty-orange crown.

Yellow-breasted Chat

FAMILY Parulidae
SPECIES *Icteria virens*
LENGTH 7½ in (19 cm)
HABITAT Dense thicket
CLUTCH SIZE 3–5

DISTRIBUTION Breeds from southern Canada across the United States. Present south of the Great Lakes in the east, but absent from most of Florida. Winters in Central America.

THE LARGE SIZE of these chats helps to identify them. Although they are the biggest of the warblers occurring in North America, their shyness means they can be difficult to observe. In both sexes, the head is gray, with white stripes on either side that run above and encircle the eyes,

WELL-HIDDEN NEST These chats conceal their nests well, often quite close to the ground.

as well as extending from the bill, separated by an intervening area of black feathering. The upperparts of the body are olive-brown; the underside is yellow.

Common Yellowthroat

FAMILY Parulidae
SPECIES *Geothlypis trichas*
LENGTH 5 in (13 cm)
HABITAT Grassland/ marshland
CLUTCH SIZE 3–6

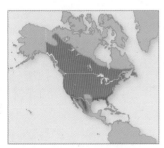

DISTRIBUTION Breeds over most of North America, apart from the far north. Resident in southern areas, occurring further south in winter.

THESE WIDELY distributed warblers tend to favor open areas of country, often grassland, where they feed on invertebrates. Even so, the birds are not very conspicuous, although the cock will usually choose to sing from a prominent position, especially at the start of the breeding period. Above, the hen is more of a brownish shade than her mate, and has buff rather than white underparts.

BLACK MASK The male Common Yellowthroat is distinguished by having a black mask and a white streak across the head.

Scarlet Tanager

FAMILY Thraupidae

SPECIES *Piranga olivacea*

LENGTH 7 in (18 cm)

HABITAT Deciduous forest

CLUTCH SIZE 3–5

DISTRIBUTION Breeding range lies in eastern North America, from Nova Scotia to the west of the Great Lakes down to Oklahoma. Overwinters in northern South America.

BRILLIANT RED PLUMAGE over much of the body contrasts with the black wings and tail of the male Scarlet Tanager in breeding plumage. The hen is easily distinguished by her greenish-yellow coloring; again the wings and tail are darker. Outside the nesting season, cocks resemble hens. Their brilliant coloration means that these tanagers are conspicuous when they are migrating, being reported over a much wider area of the country, south of their breeding haunts as they travel to their wintering grounds. They may even visit suburban areas at this stage, eating invertebrate pests, although they tend to seek food much higher in the canopy when nesting. The hen alone is responsible for incubating the eggs. These should hatch after a period of about two weeks, with the chicks fledging after a similar interval.

RED FOOD The bright coloration of the Scarlet Tanager stems from pigments ingested in its diet.

Summer Tanager

FAMILY Thraupidae

SPECIES *Piranga rubra*

LENGTH 7¾ in (20 cm)

HABITAT Pine-oak woodland/ cottonwood

CLUTCH SIZE 3–4

DISTRIBUTION Breeds in the southeast, west to Iowa, central Florida, and the Mexican border. Winters in southern Florida and into Central America.

THE HEN Summer Tanager can be easily distinguished from her mate by her orange-yellow underparts, and a greener area under the tail. The upperparts are an olive-shade. Birds from western parts of their range may be grayer, and are generally larger in size. Young birds of both sexes display a combination of red and yellow feathering at first.

ROSE COLOR The male Summer Tanager is rosy-red. As with related species, these birds have a stout bill, which reflects their varied diet.

House Sparrow

FAMILY Passeridae
SPECIES *Passer domesticus*
LENGTH 6¼ in (16 cm)
HABITAT Urban areas
CLUTCH SIZE 5–6

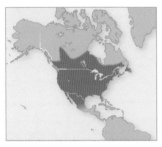

DISTRIBUTION Resident throughout the United States, as far north as the Northwest Territories in Canada. Also occurs on the south and eastern side of Newfoundland.

THESE SPARROWS were brought to North America from Europe, with the first birds being released during 1850, in Central Park, New York. The aim was to establish this lively, familiar species as a reminder of home for settlers from Europe. The House Sparrow settled in well, and started to breed, with its numbers increasing rapidly and soon forming into small flocks. Pairs will nest in a variety of locations in buildings, under the eaves for example, constructing an untidy nest, as well as breeding in tree holes in parks.

PLUMAGE This is a male with chestnut coloration prominent over the wings, and gray feathering on the crown. Hens are mainly pale brown.

White-crowned Sparrow

FAMILY Emberizidae
SPECIES *Zonotrichia leucophrys*
LENGTH 7 in (18 cm)
HABITAT Woodland/grassland
CLUTCH SIZE 3–5

DISTRIBUTION Breeds across the north to Newfoundland, and southwest to Colorado. Overwinters over a wide area.

THE WHITE-CROWNED SPARROW'S underparts are gray, and the upperparts also tend to be grayish-brown in color. The bill coloration is either yellow or pinkish. Young birds are not as brightly colored as the adults, with their crown coloration also being less distinctive. White-crowned Sparrows may build their nests at various heights, sometimes quite high off the ground. The nest takes the form of a carefully woven cup of grass, which is well-hidden from potential predators. Their eggs are pale blue in color, with variable reddish-brown spots, and are incubated by the hen on her own. It will take about two weeks for hatching to occur, and then the young will spend a further two weeks in the nest before fledging. When the young leave the nest, the cock bird assumes the duty of caring for his offspring until they are fully independent, which is likely to take another couple of weeks.

SUBURBAN BIRDS The White-crowned Sparrow is not an uncommon winter visitor in the suburbs. It will avoid areas of dense woodland.

Grasshopper Sparrow

FAMILY Emberizidae
SPECIES *Ammodramus savannarum*
LENGTH 5 in (13 cm)
HABITAT Grassland
CLUTCH SIZE 4–5

DISTRIBUTION Found in the eastern United States in the summer, northwest to southern Canada. Resident in the Gulf states and along the Mexican border, overwintering more widely here.

THIS IS A SPECIES that spends much of its time concealed in grassland. The coloration of these sparrows helps to disguise their presence here, being a mottled shade of brown, with a buff-colored breast and a whitish belly. There is a dark brown area on the crown, with a pale central stripe running down in the direction of the bill. Solitary by nature, the Grasshopper Sparrow nests on the ground as well, creating a cup-shaped nest using grass and other material. The chicks should hatch after a period of about 12 days.

BEHAVIOR The cock Grasshopper Sparrow sings loudly to attract a mate. These sparrows feed largely on seeds and also hunt for invertebrates.

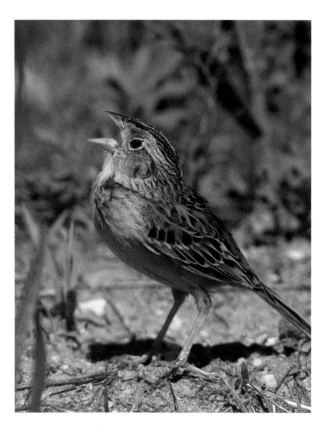

Song Sparrow

FAMILY Emberizidae
SPECIES *Melospiza melodia*
LENGTH 6 in (15 cm)
HABITAT Thicket/urban areas
CLUTCH SIZE 3–6

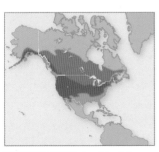

DISTRIBUTION Resident from southern Alaska right down the west coast. Breeds across southern Canada; resident in northern parts of the United States. Overwinters in the south.

HEAVY STREAKING on the underparts helps to identify these sparrows, along with the reddish-brown streaking over the back and wings. They are the most widespread of the North American species, although they are not always very conspicuous, retreating into vegetation at any hint of danger.

BACKYARD VISITOR Song Sparrows are often drawn into backyards in search of bird-table fare during spells of harsh weather.

Dark-eyed Junco

FAMILY Emberizidae

SPECIES *Junco hyemalis*

LENGTH 6¼ in (16 cm)

HABITAT Coniferous woodland/thicket

CLUTCH SIZE 3–6

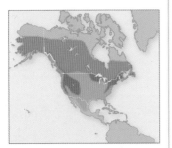

DISTRIBUTION Breeds across Canada; resident over much of the western and eastern areas of the United States. Overwinters in other parts.

THE DISTINCTIVE BLACK coloration of the eyes of this species are accentuated by the presence of dark surrounding feathering here. Its plumage coloration overall is variable, and reflects the area of an individual's origin, with six distinctive variations having been identified across its range. Birds of these different colors breed separately but may be seen overwintering together in mixed flocks.

VARIATION This is the Pink-sided form of the Dark-eyed Junco, distinguishable by the pinkish-cinnamon coloration on the sides of its body.

Snow Bunting

FAMILY Emberizidae

SPECIES *Plectrophenax nivalis*

LENGTH 6¾ in (17 cm)

HABITAT Tundra/open country

CLUTCH SIZE 4–6

DISTRIBUTION Breeds throughout the far north, including on Greenland. Resident in coastal areas of western and southern Alaska. Overwinters across southern Canada and the northern United States.

THESE BUNTINGS vary significantly in appearance through the year. It is harder to tell the sexes apart in the winter, when the black areas in the cock's plumage are replaced by buffy-brown feathering. The crown is also similarly colored at this stage, with corresponding ear patches too. Hens have more of a rusty-tan appearance in these areas. Social by nature, it is not unusual to see Snow Buntings in mixed flocks, alongside species such as longspurs and Horned Larks. They are predominately terrestrial in their habits.

SEASONAL CHANGE A male Snow Bunting in breeding plumage is recognizable by his white head and underparts, and contrasting black wings.

Indigo Bunting

FAMILY Cardinalidae
SPECIES *Passerina cyanea*
LENGTH 5½ in (14 cm)
HABITAT Woodland/brushland
CLUTCH SIZE 3–5

DISTRIBUTION Summer range extends west to southern Canada and Montana. Present in Arizona in the southwest. Overwinters in southern Florida, along the Gulf Coast to Mexico.

VIVID BLUE coloration predominates in the case of the male Indigo Bunting during the breeding season. Outside this period, their appearance is transformed to a dull brown with streaking on the chest and a hint of blue coloration remaining on the tail. It becomes impossible to distinguish the sexes at this time of year. The range of this species partly overlaps in western areas with that of the Lazuli Bunting, and it is not unknown for these birds to interbreed in this area, creating so-called hybrid offspring.

BEHAVIOR It is not uncommon for Indigo Buntings to be seen on farmland, where flocks forage for food on the ground.

Northern Cardinal

FAMILY Cardinalidae
SPECIES *Cardinalis cardinalis*
LENGTH 8¾ in (22 cm)
HABITAT Woodland/backyards
CLUTCH SIZE 3–4

DISTRIBUTION Resident throughout the southeastern area of the United States into Mexico, and also westward to central Arizona. Northern range extends right up to Nova Scotia.

THIS SPECIES is often known as the Virginian Cardinal, having been adopted as that state's national symbol. The range of these cardinals continues to expand northward and westward, as has been the case for over a century, with the first Canadian record of their presence dating back to 1901. They occur in a wide range of different environments, wherever there is cover available. Northern Cardinals may therefore enliven city parks, as well as being regular visitors to backyard bird tables, although usually preferring to feed on the ground.

GENDER DIFFERENCES Only the cock Northern Cardinal is brightly colored. Hens are easily distinguished by their olive-buff body color.

Black-headed Grosbeak

FAMILY Cardinalidae

SPECIES *Pheucticus melanocephalus*

LENGTH 8¼ in (21 cm)

HABITAT Woodland

CLUTCH SIZE 3–5

DISTRIBUTION Ranges in the summer from British Columbia down through western parts of the United States, east to the Dakotas, Nebraska, and Kansas. Overwinters in Mexico.

ONLY THE COCK in this case displays black plumage on the head. Hens are brownish above, with buff-colored underparts. The Black-headed Grosbeak has a very stocky bill, enabling these birds to crack thick-shelled seeds easily to reach the kernel inside. When breeding, these birds become

COCK BIRD The Black-headed Grosbeak nest has a relatively loose, flat, and quite fragile structure.

far more insectivorous, rearing their young mainly on invertebrates. It is the hen rather than the cock bird who lays claims to the breeding territory, driving away rivals.

Blue Grosbeak

FAMILY Cardinalidae

SPECIES *Passerina caerulea*

LENGTH 6¾ in (17 cm)

HABITAT Woodland

CLUTCH SIZE 3–4

DISTRIBUTION Across the southern United States in summer, northward to southern South Dakota and Minnesota. Absent from southern Florida. Overwinters in Central America.

IT IS VERY EASY to distinguish between the sexes in this case, because only the cock bird displays the rich blue plumage with reddish-brown wing bars. Hens in contrast are predominantly brown in color. Cock birds are not just conspicuous because of their coloration, however, but also because they often sing in the open, perched on a suitable branch.

FEEDING CHICKS Young Blue Grosbeaks are reared largely on insects, particularly grasshoppers, for which the adults forage in fields and on roadside verges.

Red-winged Blackbird

FAMILY Icteridae

SPECIES *Agelaius phoeniceus*

LENGTH 8¾ in (22 cm)

HABITAT Marshland/fields

CLUTCH SIZE 3–5

DISTRIBUTION Summer range extends up to northern Canada, with the species being found over the entire continent to the south at this stage. Overwinters in Mexico.

THIS SPECIES is one of the most common birds in North America, with a population that may be approaching 200 million individuals. It favors damp areas of countryside, particularly reedbeds. Males are easily identified by the bright red shoulder patches, with yellowish edging, which will not be very apparent when the wing is folded. Birds from the area of Central California lack this yellowish edging, with this area being completely red. Hens are easily distinguished by their brown-streaked appearance, with buff eyebrows, and again have relatively short tail feathers. Juveniles of both sexes resemble hens. Pairs nest on their own, close to the ground often in reedbeds, carefully weaving a nest that is firmly supported. The hen incubates the eggs by herself, with the chicks hatching after a period of about 12 days. They will then fledge when they are about two weeks old. After the breeding season, Red-winged Blackbirds will start to form large flocks, sometimes being seen in the company of other blackbirds at this stage. They feed on invertebrates, particularly during the summer when they are rearing their chicks, and also eat seeds.

DISPLAY Red-winged Blackbirds display with their wings held slightly away from their bodies, singing loudly.

Bobolink

FAMILY Icteridae

SPECIES *Dolichonyx oryzivorus*

LENGTH 7 in (18 cm)

HABITAT Grassland/fields

CLUTCH SIZE 4–7

DISTRIBUTION Summer range extends from southern Canada east to Nova Scotia, south in a broad band across the United States as far as Kansas. Overwinters in South America.

THE COCK BOBOLINK in breeding condition has a jet black face, with a white area on the nape of the neck, which has a yellowish hue. The rump is also white, with white edging to the wings and narrow white wing bars evident here too. It is impossible to distinguish the sexes outside the breeding season, as both then have a streaked appearance. Pairs breed on the ground in areas of grassland, constructing a cup-shaped nest here. It will take about two weeks before their eggs hatch, with the young leaving the nest after a similar period.

FALLING NUMBERS The Bobolink is not as common as it used to be in various parts of its range today.

Eastern Meadowlark

FAMILY Icteridae

SPECIES *Sturnella magna*

LENGTH 9½ in (24 cm)

HABITAT Meadow/fields

CLUTCH SIZE 3–7

DISTRIBUTION Summer range to Nova Scotia, and southwest across the United States to Arizona. Largely resident below the Great Lakes down through Texas, where some birds overwinter.

THE MARKINGS of these meadowlarks are individual. They have streaked upperparts, with prominent stripes above the eyes. There is some black on the throat, with the underparts being yellow. Markings vary between individuals, but the sexes cannot be distinguished by differences in plumage. The mottled patterning helps to conceal these birds very effectively in their grassland habitat. As their name suggests, meadowlarks are talented songsters, with cocks singing loudly in spring to attract mates. Their dome-shaped nest made of grass is well-concealed on the ground, and the hen incubates alone.

IDENTIFICATION A long, pointed bill and short tail are characteristic features of the Eastern Meadowlark, creating a rather dumpy appearance.

Brown-headed Cowbird

FAMILY Icteridae
SPECIES *Molothrus ater*
LENGTH 7½ in (19 cm)
HABITAT Woodland/farmland
CLUTCH SIZE 1 per nest

DISTRIBUTION In summer from northwestern Canada east to southern Newfoundland, and south to northern Arizona and New Mexico. Overwinters across southern parts and down the west coast.

BROWN FEATHERING on the head and chest distinguishes the cock of this species, with hens being grayish-brown. This is a parasitic species, with hens seeking out and laying in the nests of small birds such as vireos and warblers. The hen will also destroy their eggs at this stage, and other eggs laid by her own species, preventing them from hatching. The foster parents will then put all their energy into raising the young cowbird chick when it hatches in due course. Hen Brown-headed Cowbirds may lay over 70 eggs in a breeding season.

DIET Brown-headed Cowbirds spend much of their time on the ground, hunting for invertebrates and seeds.

Brewer's Blackbird

FAMILY Icteridae
SPECIES *Euphagus cyanocephalus*
LENGTH 9 in (23 cm)
HABITAT Open country/parks
CLUTCH SIZE 4–6

DISTRIBUTION Summer range extends across southwestern Canada, down to the Great Lakes, south to Colorado. Resident through much of the western United States, overwintering in the south.

AN IRIDESCENT PURPLISH head helps to identify the cock of this species, with the remainder of the body having more of a greenish tinge. During the winter months, however, this iridescence is less noticeable. Hens and young birds are grayish-brown. Nesting occurs in colonies.

ADAPTABLE Brewer's Blackbird is an adaptable species, often seen in city areas where pairs may nest in parks.

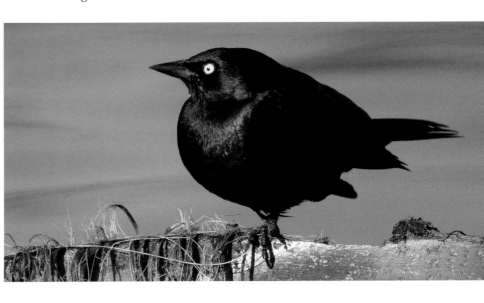

Common Grackle

FAMILY Icteridae
SPECIES *Quiscalus quiscula*
LENGTH 12½ in (32 cm)
HABITAT Fields/backyards
CLUTCH SIZE 4–6

DISTRIBUTION Southern parts of the Northwestern Territories eastward to Nova Scotia and southeast to eastern New Mexico in summer. Resident in eastern parts of United States.

THE COMMON GRACKLE is a highly adaptable species, occurring in a wide range of different habitats. Cock birds may vary in appearance, with the most commonly seen form having a bronze hue on the lower part of its body, and blue on its head and breast, but there is also a purple form, which has suffusion of this color replacing the blue.

FEEDING These grackles may eat seeds, invertebrates, amphibians, and small fish. They will also raid nests of other birds for eggs and chicks.

Baltimore Oriole

FAMILY Icteridae
SPECIES *Icterus galbula*
LENGTH 8¼ in (21 cm)
HABITAT Deciduous woodland
CLUTCH SIZE 3–6

DISTRIBUTION Eastern British Columbia to Nova Scotia, but absent from the southeastern United States in summer. Overwinters from north Carolina through Florida to southern Louisiana and Texas.

THE LINKS BETWEEN this oriole and Bullock's Oriole are such that they are sometimes considered to be a single species, referred to as the Northern Oriole. Although cock birds do differ significantly in terms of their appearance, hens and juveniles are actually very similar. As in the case of other orioles, the cocks have an attractive song. Hens sometimes sing back in an apparent reply to their partner's call, a behavior that is known as duetting.

PLUMAGE Cocks have a black cap on the head, with orange-yellow underparts and a bar of similar coloring on each wing.

White-winged Crossbill

FAMILY Fringillidae
SPECIES *Loxia leucoptera*
LENGTH 6½ in (17 cm)
HABITAT Coniferous forest
CLUTCH SIZE 3–4

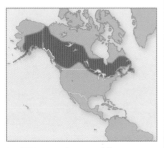

DISTRIBUTION Resident throughout Canada, except for the far north. Winters in northern parts of the United States, from northeastern Montana and North Dakota eastward.

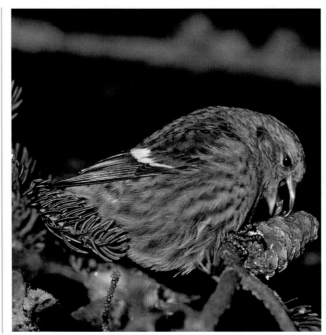

THE WHITE BARS running back from the shoulder region, and across the wing itself, help to identify this species. These areas of white plumage are smaller in immature birds, which otherwise resemble hens. On close examination, the bill of the White-winged Crossbill is relatively narrow compared with other crossbills, allowing it to feed more effectively on spruce rather than pine cones.

PLUMAGE This is a hen White-winged Crossbill. Cock birds have pinkish-red plumage, without any streaking on their bodies.

Pine Grosbeak

FAMILY Fringillidae
SPECIES *Pinicola enucleator*
LENGTH 9 in (23 cm)
HABITAT Coniferous/ deciduous woodland
CLUTCH SIZE 2–5

DISTRIBUTION Summer range from central Alaska eastward around Hudson Bay. Resident in the east to Idaho and some localities further south. Overwinters from eastern British Columbia eastward.

THESE RELATIVELY LARGE finches are usually seen in pine and spruce woodland areas, but particularly during the winter, they often wander further afield into deciduous woodland, and may be seen in parks and orchards. When breeding, a pair builds a bulky nest of twigs and other vegetation, with a softer lining for the spotted, greeny-blue eggs. The hen sits on her own, with incubation lasting for about 14 days. The young will then fledge after a period of approximately 21 days.

DISTINCTIVE FEATURE
The red coloration of the Pine Grosbeak is reminiscent of a crossbill, but these birds can be easily distinguished by their respective bill shapes.

American Goldfinch

FAMILY Fringillidae

SPECIES *Carduelis tristis*

LENGTH 5 in (13 cm)

HABITAT Fields/suburbs

CLUTCH SIZE 3–6

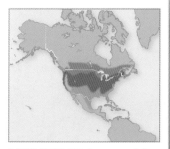

DISTRIBUTION Summer visitor to southern Canada. Resident further south, down the west coast and in central and eastern parts. Present across the southern states in winter.

THE APPEARANCE of the male American Goldfinch changes markedly through the year, since they become much more brightly colored at the start of the breeding season. Hens are also transformed, with pale yellow plumage replacing the mainly gray-colored underparts leading up to this period. Males have cinnamon-brown upperparts in winter, appearing duller, with whitish plumage on the belly.

NESTING American Goldfinches build a cup-shaped nest from grass and other vegetation. Chicks are reared on invertebrates, as well as seeds.

House Finch

FAMILY Fringillidae

SPECIES *Carpodacus mexicanus*

LENGTH 6 in (15 cm)

HABITAT Open country/ suburbs

CLUTCH SIZE 3–5

DISTRIBUTION Resident northward to southern British Columbia and other parts of southern Canada, down across the entire United States, although absent from southern Florida and southern Louisiana.

THESE FINCHES have expanded their range considerably over recent years, as they formerly only occurred in the west. Some House Finches were released in the vicinity of New York around 1940, and since then, they have prospered there, becoming widely established. Part of their adaptability stems from the fact that they will build their cup-shaped nest almost anywhere, even within buildings or hidden in the branches of trees. House Finches also eat a very varied diet, including invertebrates, seeds, and fruit.

PLUMAGE Red feathering on the head, extending to the breast, indicates that this is a cock bird. Hens have brownish, streaked plumage overall.

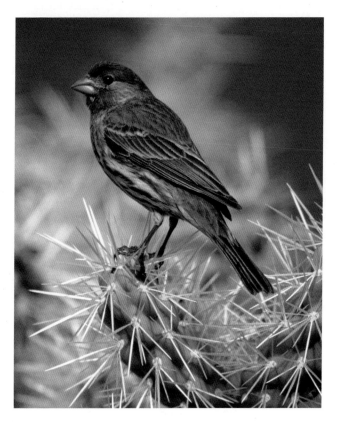

INDEX